no-fat and low-fat

guilt-free
cookbook

Consultant Editor:
Valerie Ferguson

HERMES
HOUSE

Contents

Introduction

When it comes to avoiding heart disease, recommendations are loud and clear: reduce your consumption of fat (especially saturated) and you will considerably reduce the risk of heart disease.

But what does this mean when you are shopping at the supermarket, faced with confusingly labelled foods? What exactly is saturated fat and how do we begin to limit the amount of fat we eat? These questions are answered in this book.

Cutting down on fat does not mean sacrificing taste. There is no need to forgo your favourite dishes, such as curry, lasagne or desserts, as this book shows you how to cook delicious versions using less fat. It helps you alter your approach to cooking, guiding you towards ingredients that are naturally lower in fat and cooking methods that require little, if any, additional fat. Each starter and dessert contains less than 5 g of fat per portion; main courses contain less than 10 g per portion.

You will be surprised at the variety of imaginative recipes, and each one includes nutritional information per portion. With the aid of this book you will soon be enjoying meals so tasty that it is hard to believe they are good for you.

Planning a Low Fat Diet

Reducing the fat in your diet is not difficult if you follow the advice below. A recent survey reported that men eat, on average, 102 g/3½ oz fat a day and women 73.5 g/2½ oz. Yet just 10 g/¼ oz is all you really need as long as some of it is polyunsaturated to provide the "essential" fatty acids. Fat is also necessary in the diet in order to provide the fat-soluble vitamins, A, D, E and K.

Current nutritional advice is not quite that strict, though, and suggests that we should limit our daily fat intake to no more than 33% of total calories. In real terms this means that for an average intake of 2,000 calories a day, 33% of energy would come from 660 calories or 73 g/2½ oz fat.

How To Cut Down

If you look at The Fat & Calorie Contents of Food chart, you will see how quickly you can consume too much and how you can cut down. Watch out for hidden fats in foods. For example, we tend to think of cakes as sweet foods, but usually more calories come from their fat content.

The red meats – lamb, pork and beef – are the highest in fat, so try to eat chicken and turkey more often. Always choose lean cuts of meat and remove

Above: Bread is nourishing and low in fat.

the skin and any visible fat from both meat and poultry before cooking. Avoid meat products such as sausages and pâtés. Fish, particularly types of white fish and shellfish, have a lower fat content than meat.

Fresh vegetables and fruit, with the odd exception such as avocados, are naturally low in fat (provided minimal amounts of fat are used to cook them) and vital to a healthy diet: aim to eat five portions a day. Grains such as rice, pasta, pulses and lentils all have a low fat content. Nuts are high in fat and should be eaten in small amounts. Pastry (other than filo) has no place in a low fat diet.

Cooking Methods

Grill, poach and steam foods whenever possible. If you do fry foods, use as little fat as possible. Make sauces and stews by first cooking the onions and garlic in a small quantity of stock.

Above: A selection of healthy pasta, fruit and vegetables.

Fat Facts

Fat is made up of three main types of fatty acids: saturated, mono-unsaturated and polyunsaturated.

Saturated fatty acids are believed to raise blood cholesterol levels and are thus considered to be unhealthy in excess; they are found mainly in foods of animal origin such as dairy foods (cream, full fat milk, cheese) and eggs.

Mono-unsaturated fatty acids are generally considered healthy in moderation; olives and olive oil of the Mediterranean diet are relatively high in mono-unsaturated fatty acids.

Polyunsaturated fatty acids are thought to promote a healthy blood circulation. They also provide "essential fatty acids", which are essential components of all cell membranes. Polyunsaturates are found in vegetable and seed oils and margarines derived from them, oily fish and lean meat.

Labelling

Look at labels when choosing food. Ingredients are always listed in order of quantity, so watch out for those with fat near the top as nutritional labels can be misleading.

Low fat: Contains less than half the fat of the standard product. Remember that some foods are very high in fat, so even if a product such as low fat spread has half the fat content of margarine it still contains quite a lot of fat (about 40 g per 100 g/1½ oz per 3½ oz).

Reduced fat: Contains less than 75% of the fat to be found in the standard product.

Low cholesterol: No more than 0.005% of the total fat is cholesterol.

High in polyunsaturates/low in saturates: Contains at least 35% fat of which at least 45% of the fatty acids are polyunsaturated and not more than 25% saturated.

The Fat & Calorie Content of Food

The chart shows the weight of fat and the energy content of
25 g/1 oz of various foods.

	Fat (g)	Energy
Breads, cereals,		
biscuits & preserves		
Bread, white	0.5	59 Kcals/251 kJ
Bread, wholemeal	0.6	54 Kcals/228 kJ
Rice, white, uncooked	0.3	90 Kcals/384 kJ
Pasta, white, uncooked	0.5	86 Kcals/364 kJ
Digestive biscuit	5.2	118 Kcals/494 kJ
Cake, fruit, plain, retail	3.2	89 Kcals/372 kJ
Jam	0.0	65 Kcals/273 kJ
Chocolate, plain	7.0	127 Kcals/534 kJ
Eggs & oils		
Egg, boiled (half an egg)	2.7	37 Kcals/153 kJ
Egg, white	0.0	9 Kcals/38 kJ
Egg, yolk	7.6	85 Kcals/351 kJ
Oil, sunflower	25.0	225 Kcals/924 kJ
Oil, olive	25.0	225 Kcals/924 kJ
Poultry, meat		
& meat products		
Chicken, roast, meat & skin	3.5	54 Kcals/226 kJ
Chicken, roast, meat only	1.4	37 Kcals/155 kJ
Turkey, roast, meat & skin	1.6	43 Kcals/179 kJ
Turkey, roast, meat only	0.7	35 Kcals/148 kJ
Bacon, back, grilled,		
fat trimmed	3.1	53 Kcals/223 kJ
Beef, roast, topside, lean	1.1	39 Kcals/165 kJ
Lamb, loin chop,		
grilled, lean	3.4	62 Kcals/260 kJ
Lamb, leg, roast, lean	2.4	53 Kcals/220 kJ
Pork, loin chop, grilled, lean	1.6	46 Kcals/193 kJ
Live pâté	8.2	87 Kcals/359 kJ
Pork pie, individual	6.8	94 Kcals/391 kJ
Fish		
Cod, raw	0.2	20 Kcals/84 kJ
Cod, fried in batter	3.8	61 Kcals/255 kJ
Prawns, cooked, no shell	0.2	25 Kcals/105 kJ
Salmon, tinned	1.6	38 Kcals/161 kJ
Salmon, grilled	3.3	54 Kcals/224 kJ
Trout, grilled	1.4	34 Kcals/141 kJ
Tuna, raw	1.1	34 Kcals/143 kJ
Tuna, tinned in brine	0.2	25 Kcals/106 kJ
Vegetables		
Broccoli, boiled	0.2	6 Kcals/25 kJ
Brussels sprouts, boiled	0.3	9 Kcals/37 kJ
Cauliflower, boiled	0.2	7 Kcals/29 kJ
Celery, raw	0.1	2 Kcals/7 kJ
Courgettes, boiled	0.1	5 Kcals/20 kJ
Mushrooms, raw	0.1	3 Kcals/14 kJ
Leeks, boiled	0.2	5 Kcals/22 kJ
Peas, boiled	0.2	17 Kcals/73 kJ
Peppers, raw	0.1	4 Kcals/16 kJ
Potatoes, new, boiled	0.1	19 Kcals/78 kJ
Chips, oven baked	1.1	39 Kcals/166 kJ
Chips, fried, retail	3.0	59 Kcals/246 kJ
Tomatoes, raw	0.1	4 Kcals/18 kJ
Fruit & nuts		
Apple	0.1	11 Kcals/45 kJ
Avocado	4.9	48 Kcals/196 kJ
Banana	0.1	24 Kcals/101 kJ
Dried mixed fruit	0.1	67 Kcals/281 kJ
Orange	0.0	9 Kcals/39 kJ
Peach	0.0	8 Kcals/35 kJ
Strawberries	0.0	7 Kcals/28 kJ
Almonds	14.0	153 Kcals/633 kJ
Cashews, roasted	12.7	153 Kcals/633 kJ
Coconut, desiccated	15.5	151 Kcals/623 kJ
Peanuts, roasted	13.3	150 Kcals/623 kJ
Sesame seeds	14.5	150 Kcals/618 kJ
Dairy produce		
Cream, double	12.0	112 Kcals/462 kJ
Cream, single	4.8	49 Kcals/204 kJ
Milk, whole	1.0	16 Kcals/69 kJ
Milk, semi-skimmed	0.4	11 Kcals/49 kJ
Milk, skimmed	0.0	8 Kcals/35 kJ
Margarine	20.4	185 Kcals/760 kJ
Butter	20.4	184 Kcals/758 kJ
Low fat spread (40%)	10.1	98 Kcals/401 kJ
Very low fat spread (25%)	6.3	68 Kcals/282 kJ
Crème fraîche	7.8	78 Kcals/324 kJ
Crème fraîche,		
low fat	3.8	42 Kcals/173 kJ
Fromage frais	1.8	28 Kcals/117 kJ
Fromage frais,		
very low fat	0.1	15 Kcals/62 kJ
Cheese, Cheddar	8.6	103 Kcals/427 kJ
Cheese, Cheddar,		
reduced fat	3.8	65 Kcals/273 kJ
Cheese, Edam	6.3	83 Kcals/346 kJ
Yogurt, plain, low fat	0.3	13 Kcals/54 kJ
Greek yogurt	2.3	29 Kcals/119 kJ

Low Fat Ingredients & Substitutes

There are now many lower fat versions of fats and cheeses available.

Left, clockwise from top left: olive oil, sunflower oil, buttermilk blend, sunflower light, olive oil reduced fat spread, reduced fat butter, very low fat spread.

Milk & Cheeses

Milk, cream and yogurt: Replace whole milk with skimmed or semi-skimmed. Low fat yogurt and fromage frais make excellent alternatives to cream, and can be combined with flavourings to make fillings or toppings for cakes and desserts.

Fromage frais: This is a soft cheese available in two grades: virtually fat free (0.4% fat), and creamy (7.9% fat).

Crème fraîche: Half fat crème fraîche has a fat content of 15%.

Low fat cheeses: There are a lot of reduced fat cheeses now available. Generally, harder cheeses have a higher fat content than soft cheeses. Choose mature cheese as you need less of it to give a good flavour.

Cottage cheese: A low fat soft cheese which is also available in a half fat form.

Quark: Made from fermented skimmed milk, this soft, white cheese is virtually free of fat.

Curd cheese: This is a low fat soft cheese made with either skimmed or semi-skimmed milk and can be used instead of cream cheese.

Half fat Cheddar and Red Leicester: These contain about 14% fat.

Oils

Olive oil: Use extra virgin when a recipe requires a strong flavour.

Sunflower oil: High in polyunsaturates.

Spreads

Low fat spreads are ideal for spreading on breads and tea breads, though they are not suitable for baking.

Reduced fat butter: This contains about 40% fat.

Low fat spread, rich buttermilk blend: Made with a high proportion of buttermilk, this is naturally low in fat.

Sunflower light: Contains 40% fat, plus emulsified water and milk solids.

Olive oil reduced fat spread: This spread has a better flavour than some other low fat spreads.

Very low fat spread: Contains only 20–30% fat and is not suitable for baking.

Creamy Cod Chowder

Serve this soup as a substantial starter or snack, or as a light main meal accompanied by warm, crusty wholemeal bread.

Serves 4–6

INGREDIENTS
350 g/12 oz smoked cod fillet
1 small onion, finely chopped
1 bay leaf
4 black peppercorns
900 ml/1½ pints/3¾ cups
    skimmed milk
10 ml/2 tsp cornflour
200 g/7 oz canned sweetcorn kernels
15 ml/1 tbsp chopped
    fresh parsley

2 Bring to the boil. Reduce the heat and allow to simmer very gently for 12–15 minutes or until the fish is just cooked. The fish should be opaque and of a firm texture. Do not overcook.

1 Skin the fish with a sharp knife starting at the tail end of the fillet. Put the fish into a large saucepan with the onion, bay leaf and peppercorns. Pour over the milk.

3 Using a slotted spoon, lift out the fish and flake it into large chunks. Remove and discard the bay leaf and peppercorns.

Nutritional Notes	
Energy	210 Kcals/886 kJ
Fat, total	1.3 g
Saturated fat	0.33 g
Cholesterol	45.0 mg

4 Blend the cornflour with 10 ml/ 2 tsp cold water and add to the poaching liquid in the pan. Bring to the boil and simmer for 1 minute or until slightly thickened.

5 Drain the sweetcorn kernels and add to the saucepan together with the flaked fish and chopped parsley.

6 Reheat the soup until piping hot, but do not boil. Ladle into four or six soup bowls and serve straight away.

COOK'S TIP: The flavour of the chowder improves if made a day in advance. Chill in the fridge until required, then reheat gently to prevent the fish from disintegrating.

Vegetable Minestrone with Anellini

This delicious soup, packed with vegetables, proves that flavour need not be sacrificed when fat content is reduced.

Serves 6–8

INGREDIENTS
15 ml/1 tbsp boiling water
large pinch of saffron strands
1 onion, chopped
1 leek, sliced
1 celery stick, sliced
2 carrots, diced
2–3 garlic cloves, crushed
600 ml/1 pint/2½ cups chicken stock
2 x 400 g/14 oz cans
   chopped tomatoes
50 g/2 oz/½ cup frozen peas
50 g/2 oz/½ cup soup pasta (anellini)
5 ml/1 tsp caster sugar
15 ml/1 tbsp chopped fresh parsley
15 ml/1 tbsp chopped fresh basil
salt and freshly ground
   black pepper

2 Meanwhile, put the onion, leek, celery, carrots and garlic into a pan. Add the chicken stock, bring to the boil, cover and simmer for 10 minutes.

3 Add the tomatoes, the saffron with its liquid, and the peas. Bring the soup back to the boil and add the anellini. Simmer for 10 minutes or until the pasta is tender.

1 Pour the boiling water into a small container and add the saffron strands. Leave to infuse for 10 minutes.

VARIATION: A good home-made vegetable stock can be used for this recipe, if preferred.

4 Add the sugar and seasoning. Stir in the chopped herbs just before serving.

Nutritional Notes	
Energy	85 Kcals/358 kJ
Fat, total	0.7 g
Saturated fat	0.08 g
Cholesterol	0.0 mg

Fat Free Saffron Dip

Serve this mild dip with fresh vegetable crudités – it is particularly good with florets of cauliflower.

Serves 4

INGREDIENTS
15 ml/1 tbsp boiling water
small pinch of saffron strands
200 g/7 oz/scant 1 cup fat free
    fromage frais
10 fresh chives
10 fresh basil leaves
salt and freshly ground black pepper
vegetable crudités (such as baby carrots and
    sweetcorn, cauliflower and asparagus),
    to serve

1 Pour the boiling water into a small container and add the saffron strands. Leave to infuse for 3 minutes.

2 In a mixing bowl, beat the fromage frais until smooth, then stir in the infused saffron liquid.

VARIATION: If preferred, leave out the saffron and add a squeeze of lemon or lime juice instead.

3 Use a pair of scissors to snip the chives into the dip. Tear the basil leaves into small pieces and stir them in.

4 Add salt and freshly ground black pepper to taste and stir to combine. Transfer the dip to a serving bowl and serve immediately with a variety of crisp, fresh vegetable crudités.

Nutritional Notes	
Energy	30 Kcals/129 kJ
Fat, total	0.1 g
Saturated fat	0.06 g
Cholesterol	1.0 mg

Cannellini Bean Purée with Grilled Radicchio

The slightly bitter flavours of the radicchio and chicory make a wonderful marriage with the creamy citrus bean purée.

Serves 4

INGREDIENTS
400 g/14 oz can cannellini beans
45 ml/3 tbsp low fat fromage frais
finely grated rind and juice of
   1 large orange
15 ml/1 tbsp finely chopped fresh rosemary
4 chicory heads
2 medium radicchio
15 ml/1 tbsp walnut oil
salt and freshly ground black pepper
thinly pared strips of orange rind,
   to garnish

1 Drain the beans, rinse, and drain again. Purée the beans in a blender or food processor with the fromage frais, orange rind, orange juice and rosemary. Season and set aside.

2 Using a sharp knife, cut each head of chicory in half lengthways. Cut each radicchio into eight wedges.

3 Preheat the grill. Lay out the chicory and radicchio on a baking tray and brush with walnut oil. Grill for 2–3 minutes.

4 Put the bean purée in a serving dish and arrange the grilled chicory and radicchio on top. Garnish with thin strips of orange rind and serve.

Nutritional Notes	
Energy	135 Kcals/564 kJ
Fat, total	4.3 g
Saturated fat	0.26 g
Cholesterol	0.0 mg

COOK'S TIP: If preferred, use 115 g/4 oz dried beans. Soak them in cold water overnight, drain, rinse and cover with fresh water. Boil rapidly for 10 minutes then simmer for 45 minutes or until tender.

Salmon Parcels

Delicious served with a green salad.

Makes 12

INGREDIENTS
90 g/3½ oz can red or pink salmon
15 ml/1 tbsp chopped fresh coriander
4 spring onions, finely chopped
4 sheets filo pastry, thawed if frozen
sunflower oil, for brushing

1 Preheat the oven to 200°C/400°F/Gas 6. Drain the salmon, discard any skin and bones, then flake in a bowl. Mix in the coriander and onions.

2 Place a sheet of filo pastry on a work surface and brush lightly with oil. Place another sheet on top. Cut into six 10 cm/4 in squares. Repeat with the remaining pastry, to make 12 squares in all.

3 Place a spoonful of the salmon mixture on each square. Brush the edges of the pastry with oil, then draw together, pressing to seal. Place on an oiled baking sheet and bake for 12–15 minutes until golden.

Nutritional Notes	
Energy	53 Kcals/220 kJ
Fat, total	1.5 g
Saturated fat	0.26 g
Cholesterol	2.0 mg

Tomato Cheese Tarts

Easy to make and mouth-watering.

Serves 4

INGREDIENTS
2 sheets filo pastry, thawed if frozen
1 egg white
115 g/4 oz/½ cup skimmed-milk
   soft cheese
1 handful fresh basil leaves
3 small tomatoes, sliced
salt and freshly ground black pepper

1 Preheat the oven to 200°C/400°F/Gas 6. Brush the sheets of filo pastry lightly with egg white and cut into sixteen 10 cm/4 in squares.

2 Layer the squares in twos, in eight patty tins. Spoon the cheese into the pastry cases. Season with pepper and top with some of the basil leaves.

3 Arrange tomatoes on the tarts, season with salt and pepper and bake for 10–12 minutes until golden. Serve warm garnished with basil.

Nutritional Notes	
Energy	88 Kcals/369 kJ
Fat, total	0.8 g
Saturated fat	0.13 g
Cholesterol	0.0 mg

Right: Salmon parcels (top);
Tomato Cheese Tarts

Roast Monkfish with Garlic & Fennel

A luxurious, but low fat, dish that shows monkfish at its best.

Serves 4

INGREDIENTS
1.2 kg/2½ lb monkfish tail
8 garlic cloves
15 ml/1 tbsp olive oil
2 fennel bulbs, sliced
juice of 1 lemon
1 bay leaf
salt and freshly ground black pepper
grated lemon rind, to garnish

1 Preheat the oven to 220°C/425°F/ Gas 7. With a filleting knife, cut away the thin membrane covering the outside of the fish.

2 Cut along one side of the central bone to remove the fillet. Repeat on the other side. Tie the fillets together with string. Peel and finely slice the garlic cloves. Cut incisions into the fish flesh and place the garlic slices into the incisions.

3 Heat the oil in a large, heavy-based saucepan and seal the fish on all sides.

4 Transfer the fish to a roasting tin and add the fennel, lemon juice, seasoning and bay leaf. Roast in the oven for about 20 minutes. Serve garnished with lemon rind.

Nutritional Notes	
Energy	184 Kcals/758 kJ
Fat, total	3.8 g
Saturated fat	0.65 g
Cholesterol	31.0 mg

Stuffed Plaice Rolls

Plaice fillets are a good choice for families because they are economical, easy to cook and free of bones. If you prefer, the skin can be removed.

Serves 4

INGREDIENTS
2 medium carrots, grated
1 medium courgette, grated
60 ml/4 tbsp fresh wholemeal breadcrumbs
15 ml/1 tbsp lime or lemon juice
4 plaice fillets
salt and freshly ground black pepper
boiled new potatoes,
    to serve

1 Preheat the oven to 200°C/400°F/ Gas 6. Mix together the carrots and courgettes. Stir in the breadcrumbs, lime or lemon juice and seasoning.

2 Lay the fish fillets skin side up and divide the stuffing among them, spreading it evenly.

3 Roll up to enclose the stuffing, place in an ovenproof dish and twist over some pepper. Cover and bake for about 30 minutes or until the fish flakes easily. Serve hot with new potatoes.

Nutritional Notes	
Energy	168 Kcals/713 kJ
Fat, total	2.7 g
Saturated fat	0.45 g
Cholesterol	63.0 mg

Lemon Sole in a Paper Case

New potatoes and braised celery complement the sole perfectly.

Serves 4

INGREDIENTS

4 lemon sole fillets, about 150 g/5 oz each
½ small cucumber, sliced
4 lemon slices
60 ml/4 tbsp dry white wine
150 ml/¼ pint/⅔ cup plain low fat yogurt
5 ml/1 tsp lemon juice
2 egg yolks
5 ml/1 tsp Dijon mustard
salt and freshly ground black pepper
fresh dill sprigs, to garnish

1 Preheat the oven to 180°C/350°F/ Gas 4. Cut out four heart shapes from non-stick baking parchment, each about 20 x 15 cm/8 x 6 in. Place a sole fillet on one side of each heart. Arrange the cucumber and lemon slices on top and sprinkle with wine.

2 Close the parcels by turning and twisting the edges of the paper. Put on a baking sheet and cook in the oven for 15 minutes.

3 To make the hollandaise, beat together the yogurt, lemon juice and egg yolks in a double boiler or bowl placed over a saucepan. Cook over simmering water for 15 minutes, stirring, or until thickened. Remove from the heat, stir in the mustard and season. Open the parcels, garnish with a sprig of dill and serve.

Nutritional Notes	
Energy	190 Kcals/799 kJ
Fat, total	5.2 g
Saturated fat	1.63 g
Cholesterol	181.0 mg

Halibut with Fresh Tomato & Basil Salsa

Season this dish well to bring out the delicate flavour of the fish and the fresh taste of the sauce.

Serves 4

INGREDIENTS
4 halibut fillets, about 175 g/6 oz each
15 ml/1 tbsp olive oil
fresh basil sprigs,
    to garnish

FOR THE SALSA
1 medium tomato, roughly chopped
¼ red onion, finely sliced
1 small jalapeño pepper,
    finely chopped
30 ml/2 tbsp balsamic vinegar
10 large fresh basil leaves
15 ml/1 tbsp olive oil
salt and freshly ground
    black pepper

2 Stir the basil and the olive oil into the tomato mixture. Season to taste. Cover and leave to marinate for at least 3 hours.

3 Rub the halibut fillets with the olive oil and salt and pepper. Preheat a grill or heat a barbecue and cook the fish for about 4 minutes on each side, depending on the thickness of the fillets. Baste with olive oil as necessary.

1 To make the salsa, mix together the tomato, red onion, jalapeño pepper and balsamic vinegar, in a bowl. Finely slice the basil leaves.

4 Transfer to individual serving plates, garnish with basil sprigs and serve with the salsa.

Nutritional Notes	
Energy	236 Kcals/994 kJ
Fat, total	8.9 g
Saturated fat	1.28 g
Cholesterol	61.0 mg

VARIATION: To reduce the fat content of this dish even further, you can, if you wish, omit the oil from the salsa.

Ginger & Lime Prawns

Wonderfully fresh, sharp and sweet flavours combine in this exotic low fat stir-fry. Tiger prawns make it special and ideal for entertaining.

Serves 4

INGREDIENTS
225 g/8 oz peeled raw
   tiger prawns
⅓ cucumber
10 ml/2 tsp sunflower oil
10 ml/2 tsp sesame seed oil
175 g/6 oz mangetouts, trimmed
4 spring onions,
   diagonally sliced
30 ml/2 tbsp chopped fresh coriander,
   to garnish

FOR THE MARINADE
15 ml/1 tbsp clear honey
15 ml/1 tbsp light
   soy sauce
15 ml/1 tbsp dry sherry
2 garlic cloves, crushed
small piece of fresh
   root ginger, peeled and
   finely chopped
juice of 1 lime

Nutritional Notes	
Energy	136 Kcals/569 kJ
Fat, total	6.1 g
Saturated fat	0.83 g
Cholesterol	110.0 mg

1 To make the marinade, mix all the ingredients in a bowl. Add the prawns and leave to marinate for 1–2 hours. Halve the cucumber lengthways, scoop out the seeds, then slice each half neatly into crescents; set aside.

2 Heat both oils in a large, heavy-based frying pan or wok. Drain the prawns, reserving the marinade, and stir-fry over a high heat for 4 minutes until they begin to turn pink. Add the mangetouts and cucumber and stir-fry for 2 minutes more.

COOK'S TIP: As well as using very little fat, stir-frying retains the crispness of the vegetables and their nutrients.

3 Stir in the reserved marinade, heat through, then stir in the spring onions. Serve sprinkled with coriander.

VARIATION: Other fresh green vegetables could be used for this stir-fry. Try asparagus, broccoli florets or sugar snap peas.

Sweet-&-sour Fish with Vegetables

Nutritious but low in fat, white fish is baked here in a flavoursome sauce.

Serves 4

INGREDIENTS

60 ml/4 tbsp cider vinegar
45 ml/3 tbsp light soy sauce
50 g/2 oz/¼ cup sugar
15 ml/1 tbsp tomato purée
25 ml/1½ tbsp cornflour
250 ml/8 fl oz/1 cup water
1 green pepper, seeded
   and sliced
225 g/8 oz can pineapple pieces
   in fruit juice
225 g/8 oz tomatoes, peeled
   and chopped
225 g/8 oz/3¼ cups button
   mushrooms, sliced
675 g/1½ lb chunky haddock, cod or
   hake fillets, skinned
salt and freshly ground
   black pepper

1 Preheat the oven to 180°C/350°F/ Gas 4. Mix the vinegar, soy sauce, sugar and tomato purée in a saucepan. Put the cornflour in a jug, stir in the water, then add the mixture to the saucepan, stirring well. Bring to the boil, stirring constantly until thickened. Lower the heat and simmer the sauce for 5 minutes.

2 Add the green pepper, canned pineapple pieces (with their juice), chopped tomatoes and sliced mushrooms to the sauce and heat through. Season to taste.

3 Place the fish in a single layer in a shallow ovenproof dish, pour over the sauce and cover with a lid or foil. Bake for 15–20 minutes until the fish is tender but still retains its shape. Serve immediately.

COOK'S TIP: Always check fillets of fish for bones and remove them before cooking.

Nutritional Notes	
Energy	267 Kcals/1134 kJ
Fat, total	1.7 g
Saturated fat	0.33 g
Cholesterol	61.0 mg

29

Chicken with Pineapple

This chicken has a delicate tang and is very tender. The pineapple not only tenderizes the chicken but also gives it a slight sweetness.

Serves 6

INGREDIENTS
225 g/8 oz/1 cup canned pineapple
5 ml/1 tsp ground cumin
5 ml/1 tsp ground coriander
2.5 ml/½ tsp crushed garlic
5 ml/1 tsp chilli powder
5 ml/1 tsp salt
30 ml/2 tbsp plain low fat yogurt
15 ml/1 tbsp chopped fresh coriander,
　　plus extra, to garnish
few drops of orange food
　　colouring (optional)
275 g/10 oz chicken, skinned and boned
½ red and ½ yellow or green pepper,
　　seeded and cut into
　　bite-size chunks
1 large onion, cut into
　　bite-size chunks
6 cherry tomatoes
15 ml/1 tbsp sunflower oil
salad, to serve

1 Drain the pineapple juice into a bowl. Reserve 12 chunks of pineapple and squeeze the juice from the remaining chunks into the bowl and set aside. You should have about 120 ml/4 fl oz/½ cup pineapple juice.

COOK'S TIP: If possible, use a mixture of chicken breast and thigh meat for this recipe.

2 In a large mixing bowl, blend together the cumin, ground coriander, garlic, chilli powder, salt, yogurt, fresh coriander and food colouring, if using. Pour in the reserved pineapple juice and mix together.

3 Cut the chicken into bite-size cubes, add to the yogurt and spice mixture and leave to marinate for about 1–1½ hours.

4 Preheat the grill to medium. Arrange the marinated chicken pieces, vegetables and reserved pineapple chunks alternately on six wooden or metal skewers.

Nutritional Notes	
Energy	112 Kcals/462 kJ
Fat, total	2.9 g
Saturated fat	0.51 g
Cholesterol	32.0 mg

5 Baste the kebabs with the oil, then place the skewers in a flameproof dish or grill pan. Grill, turning and basting the chicken pieces with the marinade regularly, for 15 minutes. Garnish with coriander and serve with salad.

Chicken & Barley Casserole

Enjoy low fat eating with this substantial, fruity main-course dish.

Serves 4

INGREDIENTS

4 boneless chicken breasts
15 ml/1 tbsp sunflower oil
1 large onion, sliced
1 garlic clove, crushed
3 carrots, cut into chunky sticks
2 celery sticks, thickly sliced
115 g/4 oz/⅔ cup pot or pearl barley
750 ml/1¼ pints/3 cups chicken stock
1 bay leaf
few sprigs each of fresh thyme
    and marjoram
3 eating apples
salt and freshly ground black pepper

1 Remove the skin from the chicken. Heat the oil and sauté the onion for about 5 minutes until soft.

Nutritional Notes	
Energy	360 Kcals/1520 kJ
Fat, total	5.4 g
Saturated fat	0.99 g
Cholesterol	98.0 mg

2 Stir in the garlic, carrots and celery and continue to cook over a gentle heat for a further 5 minutes.

3 Stir in the pot or pearl barley, then add the chicken breasts, stock, bay leaf and seasoning. Reserve a few herb sprigs for the garnish and add the rest to the casserole. Bring to the boil, lower the heat, cover and cook gently for 1 hour.

4 Core the apples and slice them thickly. Add to the casserole, replace the lid and cook for 15 minutes more. Serve garnished with herb sprigs.

Kashmiri Chicken Curry

Curries are considered rich and high in fat but this recipe, made with low fat yogurt, is a healthier version.

Serves 4

INGREDIENTS
10 ml/2 tsp corn oil
2 medium onions, diced
1 bay leaf
2 cloves
2.5 cm/1 in cinnamon stick
4 black peppercorns
1 baby chicken, about 675 g/1½ lb, skinned
   and cut into 8 pieces
5 ml/1 tsp garam masala
5 ml/1 tsp finely chopped fresh root ginger
5 ml/1 tsp finely chopped garlic
5 ml/1 tsp salt
5 ml/1 tsp chilli powder
15 ml/1 tbsp ground almonds
150 ml/¼ pint/⅔ cup plain low fat yogurt
2 green eating apples, peeled, cored and
   roughly sliced
15 ml/1 tbsp chopped fresh coriander
15 g/½ oz/2 tbsp flaked almonds, lightly
   toasted, and fresh coriander leaves, to garnish

1 Heat the oil in a heavy-based frying pan and fry the onions with the bay leaf, cloves, cinnamon and peppercorns for about 3–5 minutes. Add the chicken pieces and continue to stir-fry for at least 3 minutes.

2 Lower the heat and add the garam masala, ginger, garlic, salt, chilli powder and ground almonds and continue to stir-fry for 2–3 minutes.

3 Pour in the yogurt and cook, stirring, for a couple more minutes. Add the apples and chopped coriander, cover and simmer for 10–15 minutes or until the chicken is cooked.

4 Sprinkle in half the flaked almonds then serve immediately, garnished with the remaining flaked almonds and whole coriander leaves.

Nutritional Notes	
Energy	208 Kcals/870 kJ
Fat, total	8.1 g
Saturated fat	1.2 g
Cholesterol	69.0 mg

Low Fat Lasagne

This classic pasta dish can be just as tempting and delicious when made with the minimum of fat.

Serves 6–8

INGREDIENTS
1 large onion, chopped
2 garlic cloves, crushed
500 g/1¼ lb minced turkey meat
450 g/1 lb carton passata (smooth, thick, sieved tomatoes)
5 ml/1 tsp dried mixed herbs
225 g/8 oz frozen leaf spinach, defrosted
200 g/7 oz non-pre-cook lasagne verdi
200 g/7 oz/scant 1 cup low fat cottage cheese
salt and freshly ground black pepper
mixed salad, to serve

FOR THE SAUCE
25 g/1 oz/2 tbsp low fat spread
25 g/1 oz/¼ cup plain flour
300 ml/½ pint/1¼ cups skimmed milk
1.5 ml/¼ tsp freshly grated nutmeg
25 g/1 oz/⅓ cup freshly grated Parmesan cheese

1 Put the chopped onion, garlic and minced turkey into a non-stick saucepan. Brown quickly for 5 minutes, stirring with a wooden spoon to separate the pieces.

2 Add the sieved tomatoes, herbs and seasoning. Bring to the boil, cover and simmer for 30 minutes.

3 To make the sauce, put all the ingredients, except the Parmesan cheese, into a saucepan. Heat to thicken, whisking constantly until bubbling and smooth. Adjust the seasoning, add most of the Parmesan to the sauce and stir.

4 Preheat the oven to 190°C/375°F/Gas 5. Lay the spinach leaves out on kitchen paper and pat dry.

5 Layer the turkey mixture, dried lasagne, cottage cheese and spinach in a 2 litre/3½ pint/9 cup ovenproof dish, starting and ending with a layer of turkey mixture.

6 Spoon the sauce over the top to cover evenly and sprinkle with Parmesan. Bake for 45–50 minutes or until bubbling and golden brown. Serve with a mixed salad.

Nutritional Notes	
Energy	339 Kcals/1432 kJ
Fat, total	6.3 g
Saturated fat	2.03 g
Cholesterol	67.0 mg

Spiced Lamb & Vegetable Couscous

A range of vegetables is cooked with the meat, using very little fat, to create this tasty stew which is served on a bed of couscous.

Serves 6

INGREDIENTS
30 ml/2 tbsp plain flour
350 g/12 oz lean lamb fillet, cut into
    2 cm/¾ in cubes
10 ml/2 tsp sunflower oil
1 onion, chopped
2 garlic cloves, crushed
1 red pepper, seeded and diced
5 ml/1 tsp ground coriander
5 ml/1 tsp ground cumin
5 ml/1 tsp ground allspice
2.5 ml/½ tsp hot chilli powder
300 ml/½ pint/1¼ cups lamb stock
400 g/14 oz can chopped tomatoes
225 g/8 oz carrots, sliced
175 g/6 oz parsnips, sliced
175 g/6 oz courgettes, sliced
175 g/6 oz/2½ cups closed cup
    mushrooms, quartered
225 g/8 oz/2 cups frozen
    broad beans
115 g/4 oz/⅔ cup sultanas
450 g/1 lb/2⅔ cups quick-cook couscous
salt and freshly ground black pepper
fresh coriander, to garnish

1 Season the flour. Toss the lamb in the flour. Heat the oil in a large, non-stick saucepan and add the lamb, onion, garlic and red pepper. Cook for 5 minutes, stirring frequently.

2 Add any remaining flour to the pan along with the spices and cook for 1 minute, stirring.

3 Gradually add the stock, stirring continuously, then add the chopped tomatoes and sliced carrots and parsnips. Stir to mix well.

Nutritional Notes	
Energy	438 Kcals/1836 kJ
Fat, total	8.0 g
Saturated fat	2.52 g
Cholesterol	0.0 mg

4 Bring to the boil, stirring, then cover and simmer for 30 minutes, stirring from time to time.

5 Add the sliced courgettes, mushrooms, broad beans and sultanas. Cover, return to the boil and simmer, stirring occasionally, for a further 20–30 minutes, until the lamb and vegetables are tender. Season to taste.

6 Meanwhile, soak the couscous and steam in a lined colander over a pan of boiling water for about 20 minutes, until cooked, or according to the packet instructions. Pile the cooked couscous on to a warmed serving platter or individual plates and top with the spiced lamb and vegetable stew. Garnish with fresh coriander and serve immediately.

Minted Lamb

Ask your butcher to remove the bone from a leg of lamb so that the meat can be sliced easily.

Serves 4

INGREDIENTS
450 g/1 lb boneless lean leg of lamb,
    cut into 5 mm/¼ in thick slices
30 ml/2 tbsp chopped fresh mint
½ lemon, roughly chopped
300 ml/½ pint/1¼ cups plain
    low fat yogurt
5 ml/1 tsp sunflower oil
salt and freshly ground
    black pepper
grated lemon rind, lemon slices and
    fresh mint sprigs, to garnish

1 Place the lamb in a bowl and sprinkle over half the mint. Season well and leave for 20 minutes.

2 Put the lemon into a food processor. Process until finely chopped. Empty it into a bowl, then stir in the yogurt and remaining mint.

3 Heat a wok, then add the oil. When the oil is hot, add the lamb and stir-fry for 4–5 minutes until cooked. Serve with yogurt dressing, garnished with lemon rind, lemon slices and mint sprigs.

Nutritional Notes	
Energy	225 Kcals/924 kJ
Fat, total	9.9 g
Saturated fat	4.41 g
Cholesterol	3.0 mg

Oriental Beef

Cut diagonally across the beef to make thin slices for this exquisite dish.

Serves 4

INGREDIENTS
450 g/1 lb lean rump steak, sliced into
    thin pieces
6 radishes
10 cm/4 in piece cucumber
1 piece stem ginger
15 ml/1 tbsp sunflower oil
4 radishes, to garnish

FOR THE MARINADE
2 garlic cloves, crushed
60 ml/4 tbsp dark soy sauce
30 ml/2 tbsp dry sherry
10 ml/2 tsp soft dark
    brown sugar

1 Mix all the marinade ingredients together in a bowl.

2 Place the beef in a larger bowl, pour over the marinade and leave to marinate overnight.

3 To make the relish, chop the radishes and cucumber into matchsticks and the ginger into small matchsticks. Mix well together in a bowl.

4 Heat the oil in a wok. Add the meat and marinade and stir-fry for 3–4 minutes. Serve with the relish, and garnish with a radish on each plate.

Nutritional Notes	
Energy	205 Kcals/860 kJ
Fat, total	7.5 g
Saturated fat	2.22 g
Cholesterol	66.0 mg

Mixed Vegetables with Aromatic Seeds

Spices transform everyday vegetables into a tasty main-course dish with a low fat content.

Serves 6

INGREDIENTS
675 g/1½ lb small new potatoes
1 small cauliflower
175 g/6 oz/1 cup French beans
115 g/4 oz/1 cup frozen peas
1 small piece fresh root ginger
30 ml/2 tbsp sunflower oil
10 ml/2 tsp cumin seeds
10 ml/2 tsp black mustard seeds
30 ml/2 tbsp sesame seeds
juice of 1 lemon
salt and freshly ground black pepper
fresh coriander, to garnish (optional)

1 Scrub the potatoes, break the cauliflower into small florets and trim and halve the French beans.

VARIATION: Other vegetables could be used, such as courgettes, leeks or broccoli.

2 Cook the vegetables in separate pans of lightly salted boiling water until tender, allowing 15–20 minutes for the potatoes, 8–10 minutes for the cauliflower and 4–5 minutes for the beans and peas. Drain thoroughly.

3 Using a small, sharp knife, peel and finely chop the fresh ginger. Heat the oil, add the ginger and seeds and fry until the seeds start to pop.

4 Add the vegetables and stir-fry for 2–3 minutes. Sprinkle over the lemon juice and season with freshly ground pepper. Garnish with fresh coriander, if using, and serve.

Nutritional Notes	
Energy	193 Kcals/809 kJ
Fat, total	8.5 g
Saturated fat	0.96 g
Cholesterol	0.0 mg

Vegetable Paella

A delicious change from the more traditional seafood-based paella.

Serves 6

INGREDIENTS
1 onion, chopped
2 garlic cloves, crushed
225 g/8 oz/2 cups leeks, sliced
3 celery sticks, chopped
1 red pepper, seeded and sliced
2 courgettes, sliced
175 g/6 oz/2½ cups brown cap
   mushrooms, sliced
175 g/6 oz/1½ cups frozen peas
450 g/1 lb/2¼ cups long grain brown rice
400 g/14 oz can cannellini beans,
   rinsed and drained
900 ml/1½ pints/3¾ cups vegetable stock
60 ml/4 tbsp dry white wine
few saffron strands
225 g/8 oz/2 cups cherry tomatoes, halved
45–60 ml/3–4 tbsp chopped fresh
   mixed herbs
salt and freshly ground black pepper
cherry tomatoes and celery leaves, to garnish

1 Put the onion, garlic, leeks, celery, red pepper, courgettes and mushrooms in a large saucepan and mix together.

2 Add the peas, rice, cannellini beans, vegetable stock, wine and saffron strands, and stir well to mix.

3 Bring to the boil, stirring, then simmer, for about 35 minutes uncovered, stirring occasionally, until almost all the liquid has been absorbed and the rice is tender.

Nutritional Notes	
Energy	391 Kcals/1659 kJ
Fat, total	2.4 g
Saturated fat	0.17 g
Cholesterol	0.0 mg

4 Stir in the tomatoes, chopped herbs and seasoning. Serve garnished with cherry tomatoes and celery leaves.

VARIATION: You could also use chick-peas, haricot beans or black-eyed beans in this recipe.

Tofu Stir-fry with Egg Noodles

This meatless dish is an excellent way of cutting down on fat without lowering protein intake – and it tastes wonderful too.

Serves 4

INGREDIENTS
225 g/8 oz firm smoked tofu
45 ml/3 tbsp dark soy sauce
30 ml/2 tbsp sherry or vermouth
3 leeks, thinly sliced
2.5 cm/1 in piece fresh root ginger, peeled and finely grated
1–2 red chillies, seeded and sliced into rings
1 small red pepper, seeded and thinly sliced
150 ml/¼ pint/⅔ cup vegetable stock
10 ml/2 tsp runny honey
10 ml/2 tsp cornflour
225 g/8 oz medium egg noodles
salt and freshly ground black pepper

2 Put the leeks, ginger, chilli, red pepper and stock into a frying pan. Bring to the boil and cook quickly for 2–3 minutes until just soft.

3 Strain the tofu, reserving the marinade. Mix the honey and cornflour into the marinade.

4 Put the egg noodles into a large pan of boiling water and leave to stand for about 6 minutes until cooked (or follow the instructions on the packet).

5 Heat a non-stick frying pan and quickly fry the tofu until lightly golden brown on all sides.

1 Cut the tofu into 2 cm/¾ in cubes. Put it into a bowl with the soy sauce and sherry or vermouth. Toss to coat each piece and leave to marinate for about 30 minutes.

Nutritional Notes	
Energy	329 Kcals/1390 kJ
Fat, total	7.7 g
Saturated fat	0.64 g
Cholesterol	0.0 mg

6 Transfer the tofu to a saucepan and add the vegetable mixture and marinade. Heat and stir until the liquid is thick and glossy and adjust the seasoning if necessary. Spoon on to the drained egg noodles and serve at once.

Pasta Primavera

Serves 4

INGREDIENTS

225 g/8 oz thin asparagus spears, cut in half
115 g/4 oz mangetouts, trimmed
115 g/4 oz whole baby sweetcorn
225 g/8 oz whole baby carrots, trimmed
1 small red pepper, seeded and chopped
8 spring onions, sliced
225 g/8 oz torchietti
150 ml/¼ pint/⅔ cup low fat cottage cheese
150 ml/¼ pint/⅔ cup plain low fat yogurt
15 ml/1 tbsp lemon juice
15 ml/1 tbsp chopped fresh parsley
15 ml/1 tbsp snipped fresh chives
skimmed milk (optional)
salt and freshly ground black pepper

1 Cook the asparagus in boiling, salted water for 3–4 minutes. Cook the mangetouts for 2 minutes.

2 Cook the remaining vegetables in the same way until tender. Drain all the vegetables and rinse under cold water.

3 Cook the pasta in a large pan of boiling, salted water until *al dente*. Drain thoroughly.

4 Process the cottage cheese, yogurt, lemon juice, herbs and seasoning in a food processor. Thin with skimmed milk, if necessary. Put into a large pan with the pasta and vegetables, heat gently and toss carefully. Serve.

Nutritional Notes	
Energy	307 Kcals/1299 kJ
Fat, total	3.0 g
Saturated fat	0.4 g
Cholesterol	2.0 mg

Sweet-&-sour Peppers

A zingy, fatless dressing is the secret behind this colourful pasta dish.

Serves 4–6

INGREDIENTS

1 red, 1 yellow and 1 orange pepper,
   quartered and seeded
225 g/8 oz pasta bows (farfalle)
salt and freshly ground
   black pepper
shavings of Parmesan cheese,
   to serve (optional)

FOR THE CAPER DRESSING

1 garlic clove, crushed
30 ml/2 tbsp capers
30 ml/2 tbsp raisins
5 ml/1 tsp wholegrain mustard
rind and juice of 1 lime
5 ml/1 tsp runny honey
30 ml/2 tbsp chopped
   fresh coriander

1 Cook the peppers in boiling water for 10–15 minutes until tender. Drain and rinse. Peel away the skin and cut the flesh into strips lengthways. In a bowl, whisk together the dressing ingredients and seasoning.

2 Cook the pasta in a large pan of boiling, salted water until *al dente*. Drain thoroughly. Return the pasta to the pan and add the peppers and caper dressing. Heat gently and toss to mix. Serve with Parmesan shavings, if using.

Nutritional Notes	
Energy	253 Kcals/1076 kJ
Fat, total	1.6 g
Saturated fat	0.2 g
Cholesterol	0.0 mg

Vegetable Biryani

This exotic dish made from everyday ingredients will be appreciated by vegetarians and meat-eaters alike who are looking to cut down on fat.

Serves 4–6

INGREDIENTS

175 g/6 oz/scant 1 cup long grain rice
2 cloves
seeds of 2 cardamom pods
450 ml/¾ pint/scant 2 cups
   vegetable stock
2 garlic cloves
1 small onion, roughly chopped
5 ml/1 tsp cumin seeds
5 ml/1 tsp ground coriander
2.5 ml/½ tsp ground turmeric
2.5 ml/½ tsp chilli powder
1 large potato, cut into 2.5 cm/1 in cubes
2 carrots, sliced
½ cauliflower, broken into florets
50 g/2 oz/½ cup French beans, cut into
   2.5 cm/1 in lengths
30 ml/2 tbsp chopped fresh coriander
30 ml/2 tbsp lime juice
salt and freshly ground black pepper
1 fresh coriander sprig, to garnish

1 Put the rice, cloves and cardamom seeds into a large, heavy-based saucepan. Pour over the stock and bring to the boil.

Nutritional Notes	
Energy	244 Kcals/1033 kJ
Fat, total	1.7 g
Saturated fat	0.07 g
Cholesterol	0.0 mg

2 Reduce the heat, cover and simmer gently for 20 minutes or until all the stock has been absorbed.

3 Meanwhile put the garlic, onion, cumin seeds, ground coriander, turmeric, chilli powder and seasoning into a blender or coffee grinder, together with 30 ml/2 tbsp water. Blend to a paste.

4 Preheat the oven to 180°C/350°F/ Gas 4. Spoon the spicy paste into a flameproof casserole and cook gently over a low heat for 2 minutes, stirring occasionally.

5 Add the potato, carrots, cauliflower, beans and 90 ml/6 tbsp water to the casserole and mix thoroughly with the spice mixture. Cover and cook over a low heat for a further 12 minutes, stirring occasionally. Add the chopped fresh coriander.

6 Spoon the rice over the vegetables and then sprinkle over the lime juice. Cover the casserole and cook in the oven for 25 minutes or until the vegetables are tender. Fluff up the rice with a fork, garnish with a sprig of fresh coriander, and serve.

Carrot Mousse with Mushroom Sauce

This impressive yet easy-to-make mousse makes low fat eating a pleasure. Brown rice and leeks make ideal accompaniments.

Serves 4

INGREDIENTS
350 g/12 oz carrots,
   roughly chopped
1 small red pepper, seeded and
   roughly chopped
45 ml/3 tbsp vegetable stock or water
2 eggs
1 egg white
115 g/4 oz/½ cup quark or low fat
   soft cheese
15 ml/1 tbsp chopped fresh tarragon
salt and freshly ground black pepper
1 fresh tarragon sprig,
   to garnish

FOR THE MUSHROOM SAUCE
25 g/1 oz/2 tbsp low fat spread
175 g/6 oz/2½ cups
   mushrooms, sliced
30 ml/2 tbsp plain flour
250 ml/8 fl oz/1 cup
   skimmed milk

1 Preheat the oven to 190°C/375°F/ Gas 5. Line the bases of four 150 ml/ ¼ pint/⅔ cup dariole moulds with non-stick baking parchment. Put the carrots and red pepper in a saucepan with the vegetable stock or water. Cover and cook for 5 minutes or until tender. Drain well.

2 Lightly beat the eggs and egg white together. Mix with the quark or low fat soft cheese. Season to taste. Purée the cooked vegetables in a food processor. Add the cheese mixture and process briefly until smooth. Stir in the chopped tarragon.

3 Divide the carrot mixture among the prepared moulds and cover with foil. Place in a roasting tin half filled with hot water. Bake for 35 minutes or until set.

4 To make the mushroom sauce, melt 15 g/½ oz/1 tbsp of the low fat spread in a frying pan. Add the mushrooms and sauté for 5 minutes until soft.

5 Put the remaining low fat spread in a saucepan with the flour and milk. Cook over a medium heat, stirring all the time, until thickened. Add the mushrooms and season.

6 Turn out each mousse on to a serving plate. Spoon over the sauce and serve, garnished with tarragon.

Nutritional Notes	
Energy	188 Kcals/788 kJ
Fat, total	6.0 g
Saturated fat	2.0 g
Cholesterol	101.0 mg

Blackcurrant Sorbet

This vibrant and intensely flavoured sorbet is completely fat free.

Serves 4–6

INGREDIENTS
90 g/3½ oz/½ cup caster sugar
120 ml/4 fl oz/½ cup water
500 g/1¼ lb/4½ cups blackcurrants
juice of ½ lemon
15 ml/1 tbsp egg white

1 In a small saucepan over a medium-high heat, bring the caster sugar and water to the boil, stirring the mixture continuously until the sugar dissolves. Boil the syrup for 2 minutes, then remove the pan from the heat and set aside to cool.

2 Remove the blackcurrants from the stalks, by pulling them through the tines of a fork.

Nutritional Notes	
Energy	135 Kcals/573 kJ
Fat, total	0 g
Saturated fat	0 g
Cholesterol	0.0 mg

3 In a food processor fitted with the metal blade, process the blackcurrants and lemon juice until smooth. Alternatively, chop the blackcurrants coarsely, then add the lemon juice. Mix in the sugar syrup.

4 Press the purée through a sieve to remove the seeds. Pour the blackcurrant purée into a non-metallic, freezerproof dish. Cover with clear film and freeze until the sorbet is nearly firm, but still slushy.

5 Cut the sorbet into pieces and put into the food processor. Process until smooth, then, with the machine running, add the egg white and process until well mixed. Tip the sorbet back into the dish and freeze until almost firm.

6 Chop the sorbet again and process until smooth. Serve immediately or freeze, covered, for up to 1 week. Allow to soften for 5–10 minutes at room temperature before serving.

Spiced Pear & Blueberry Parcels

This combination makes a delicious dessert for a summer's evening.

Serves 4

INGREDIENTS
4 firm, ripe pears
30 ml/2 tbsp fresh lemon juice
15 ml/1 tbsp melted butter
150 g/5 oz/1¼ cups blueberries
60 ml/4 tbsp light muscovado sugar
freshly ground black pepper

1 Preheat the oven to 180°C/350°F/ Gas 4. Peel the pears thinly and cut them in half lengthways. Scoop out the core from each half using a teaspoon and a sharp knife.

COOK'S TIP: If you wish to assemble the dessert in advance, place a layer of greaseproof paper inside the parcel, otherwise the acid in the lemon juice may react with the foil and taint the flavour.

2 Brush the pears with lemon juice to prevent them from turning brown while in contact with the air.

3 Cut four squares of double-thickness foil, large enough to wrap the pears, and brush them with melted butter. Place two pear halves on each, cut-side upwards. Gather the foil up around the pears to hold them level while you fill them.

4 Mix the blueberries and sugar together and spoon on top of the pears. Sprinkle with pepper. Wrap the foil over and bake for 20–25 minutes. Alternatively, cook them on a fairly hot barbecue. Serve immediately.

Nutritional Notes	
Energy	160 Kcals/672 kJ
Fat, total	3.3 g
Saturated fat	1.95 g
Cholesterol	9.0 mg

Cherry Pancakes

These pancakes are virtually fat free, but just as scrumptious as traditional ones. Serve with a spoonful of plain low fat yogurt or fromage frais.

Serves 4

INGREDIENTS
50 g/2 oz/½ cup plain flour
50 g/2 oz/½ cup plain wholemeal flour
pinch of salt
1 egg white
150 ml/¼ pint/⅔ cup skimmed milk
150 ml/¼ pint/⅔ cup water
sunflower oil, for frying

FOR THE FILLING
425 g/15 oz can black cherries in juice
7.5 ml/1½ tsp arrowroot

1 Sift the flours and salt into a bowl, adding any bran left in the sieve to the bowl at the end.

2 Make a well in the centre of the flour and add the egg white. Gradually beat in the milk and water, whisking hard until all the liquid is incorporated and the batter is smooth and bubbly.

3 Heat a small amount of oil in a non-stick pan until very hot and pour in just enough batter to cover the base.

4 Swirl the pan to cover the base evenly. Cook until the pancake is set and golden and then turn it to cook the other side. Remove to a sheet of kitchen paper. Cook the remaining batter, to make about eight pancakes. Stack them between sheets of kitchen paper.

5 To make the filling, drain the cherries, reserving the juice. Blend about 30 ml/2 tbsp of the juice with the arrowroot in a saucepan. Stir in the rest of the juice. Heat gently, stirring, until boiling. Stir over a moderate heat for about 2 minutes until thickened and clear.

Nutritional Notes	
Energy	162 Kcals/686 kJ
Fat, total	2.1 g
Saturated fat	0.28 g
Cholesterol	1.0 mg

6 Add the cherries and stir until thoroughly heated. Spoon the cherries into the pancakes and fold them into quarters before serving.

COOK'S TIP: If fresh cherries are in season, cook them gently in enough apple juice just to cover them, and then thicken the juice with arrowroot as in Step 5.

Nectarine Amaretto Cake

Try this delicious cake with low fat fromage frais for dessert. The syrup makes it moist, but not soggy.

Serves 8

INGREDIENTS
3 eggs, separated
175 g/6 oz/generous ¾ cup caster sugar
grated rind and juice of 1 lemon
50 g/2 oz/⅓ cup semolina
40 g/1½ oz/⅓ cup ground almonds
25 g/1 oz/¼ cup plain flour
60 ml/4 tbsp apricot jam
a squeeze of lemon juice
2 nectarines or peaches,
   halved and stoned

FOR THE SYRUP
75 g/3 oz/6 tbsp caster sugar
90 ml/6 tbsp water
30 ml/2 tbsp Amaretto liqueur

1 Preheat the oven to 180°C/350°F/ Gas 4. Grease a 20 cm/8 in round, loose-bottomed cake tin. Whisk the egg yolks, caster sugar, lemon rind and juice in a bowl until thick, pale and creamy. Fold in the semolina, almonds and flour until smooth.

2 Whisk the egg whites in a greasefree bowl until fairly stiff. Using a metal spoon, stir a generous spoonful of the whites into the semolina mixture to lighten it, then fold in the remaining egg whites. Spoon the mixture into the prepared cake tin.

3 Bake for 30–35 minutes until the centre of the cake springs back when lightly pressed. Remove from the oven and carefully loosen around the edge with a palette knife. Prick the top of the cake with a skewer and leave to cool slightly in the tin.

4 To make the syrup, heat the sugar and water in a small pan, stirring until dissolved, then boil without stirring for 2 minutes. Add the Amaretto liqueur and drizzle slowly over the cake.

5 Put the apricot jam and lemon juice in a small pan and heat until runny. Press through a sieve, return to the pan and warm through gently.

6 Remove the cake from the, tin and transfer it to a serving plate. Slice the nectarines or peaches, arrange them in an overlapping pattern over the top of the cake. Brush with the warm apricot glaze. Serve.

Nutritional Notes	
Energy	258 Kcals/1091 kJ
Fat, total	5.0 g
Saturated fat	0.80 g
Cholesterol	72.0 mg

Chestnut & Orange Roulade

Low in fat but still luxurious, this makes an ideal special-occasion dessert.

Serves 8

INGREDIENTS
3 eggs, separated
115 g/4 oz/generous ½ cup caster sugar
½ x 439 g/15½ oz can unsweetened
  chestnut purée
grated rind and juice of 1 orange
icing sugar, for dusting

FOR THE FILLING
225 g/8 oz/1 cup low fat soft cheese
15 ml/1 tbsp clear honey
1 orange

1 Preheat the oven to 180°C/350°F/
Gas 4. Grease a 30 x 20 cm/12 x 8 in
Swiss roll tin and line with non-stick
baking parchment. Whisk the egg
yolks and sugar in a bowl until thick.

2 Put the chestnut purée in a separate
bowl. Whisk in the orange rind and
juice, then whisk the flavoured
chestnut purée into the egg mixture.

3 Whisk the egg whites in a greasefree bowl until fairly stiff. Using a
metal spoon, stir a generous spoonful
of the whites into the chestnut mixture
to lighten it, then fold in the rest.

4 Spoon the roulade mixture into the
prepared tin and bake for 30 minutes
until firm. Cool for 5 minutes, then
cover with a clean, damp dish towel,
and leave until completely cold.

5 To make the filling, put the soft
cheese in a bowl with the honey.
Finely grate the orange rind and add
to the bowl. Peel away all the pith
from the orange, cut the fruit into
segments, then chop roughly. Beat any
juice into the cheese mixture, then
mix in the chopped orange.

Nutritional Notes	
Energy	201 Kcals/851 kJ
Fat, total	3.2 g
Saturated fat	0.77 g
Cholesterol	72.0 mg

6 Sprinkle a sheet of greaseproof paper thickly with icing sugar. Carefully turn the roulade out on to the paper, then peel off the lining paper. Spread the filling over the roulade and roll up like a Swiss roll. Transfer to a plate and dust with more icing sugar before serving.

This edition is published by Hermes House

Hermes House is an imprint of Anness Publishing Ltd
Hermes House, 88–89 Blackfriars Road, London SE1 8HA
tel. 020 7401 2077; fax 020 7633 9499; info@anness.com

A CIP catalogue record for this book is available from the British Library.

Publisher: Joanna Lorenz
Editor: Valerie Ferguson
Series Designer: Bobbie Colgate Stone
Designer: Andrew Heath
Production Controller: Joanna King
Recipes contributed by: Catherine Atkinson, Carole Clements, Christine France,
Silvano Franco, Carole Handslip, Shehzad Hussain, Sue Maggs, Annie Nichols,
Maggie Pannell, Anne Sheasby, Liz Trigg, Elizabeth Wolf-Cohen
Photography: William Adams-Lingwood, Karl Adamson, David Armstrong, James Duncan,
Michelle Garrett, Amanda Heywood, David Jordan, Don Last, Peter Reilly.

Previously published as *Low Fat Cooking*

Notes:
For all recipes, quantities are given in both metric and imperial measures and,
where appropriate, measures are also given in standard cups and spoons.
Follow one set, but not a mixture, because they are not interchangeable.
Standard spoon and cup measures are level.
1 tsp = 5 ml   1 tbsp = 15 ml
1 cup = 250 ml/8 fl oz
Australian standard tablespoons are 20 ml.
Australian readers should use 3 tsp in place of
1 tbsp for measuring small quantities of gelatine, cornflour, salt etc.
Medium eggs are used unless otherwise stated.

1 3 5 7 9 10 8 6 4 2

Festive Breakfast Casserole

Start to Finish: 3 hours
Prep: 15 minutes **Refrigerate:** 2 hours
Bake: 45 minutes

8	ounces bulk pork sausage
12	slices white bread, cut in cubes (about 6 cups)
1½	cups shredded Cheddar cheese (6 ounces)
1	cup Pace® Picante Sauce *or* Chunky Salsa
4	eggs
¾	cup milk

1. Cook the sausage in a 10-inch skillet over medium-high heat until the sausage is well browned, stirring frequently to break up meat. Pour off any fat. Remove the sausage with a slotted spoon and put it in a 12×8×2-inch shallow baking dish. Top with the bread and cheese.

2. Beat the picante sauce, eggs and milk with a whisk or a fork in a medium bowl. Pour over the bread mixture. Cover and refrigerate for at least 2 hours or overnight.

3. Uncover the dish. Bake at 350°F. for 45 minutes or until a knife inserted in the center comes out clean.

Makes: 6 servings

Nutritional Values Per Serving: Calories 350, Fat 20g, Saturated Fat 9g, Cholesterol 189mg, Sodium 951mg, Carbohydrate 22g, Fiber 2g, Protein 19g

Spice Up Your Morning

5

Border Eggs Benedict

Start to Finish: 20 minutes
Prep: 5 minutes
Cook: 15 minutes

- **4** slices Canadian bacon
- **1½** cups Pace® Picante Sauce
- **½** teaspoon ground cumin
- **4** eggs
- **2** packages (3 ounces *each*) cream cheese, cut into cubes
- **2** English muffins, split and toasted
- **1** tablespoon chopped fresh cilantro leaves

1. Cook the bacon in an 8-inch skillet over medium heat until it's lightly browned.

2. Heat the picante sauce and cumin in a 10-inch skillet over medium-high heat to a boil. Crack the eggs and add to the skillet one at a time. Reduce the heat to low. Cook eggs to desired doneness. Remove the eggs with a slotted spoon and keep them warm. Add the cream cheese to the skillet. Cook and stir until the cheese melts.

3. Top each muffin half with **1** slice bacon and **1** egg. Divide the picante sauce mixture among the egg sandwiches and sprinkle with the cilantro.

Makes: 4 servings

Nutritional Values Per Serving:
Calories 363,
Fat 22g,
Saturated Fat 12g,
Cholesterol 272mg,
Sodium 1441mg,
Carbohydrate 21g,
Fiber 4g,
Protein 17g

Spice Up Your Morning

Scrambled Tortilla Eggs

Start to Finish: 20 minutes
Prep: 5 minutes
Cook: 15 minutes

8 **eggs**
1 **cup Pace® Picante Sauce**
2 **tablespoons butter**
1 **cup shredded Monterey Jack cheese (4 ounces)**
1 **cup crumbled tortilla chips**
1 **large avocado, peeled, pitted and sliced**

1. Beat the eggs and **2 tablespoons** of the picante sauce with a whisk or a fork in a medium bowl.

2. Heat the butter in a 12-inch skillet over medium heat. Add the egg mixture. Cook and stir with a fork until the eggs are set but still moist. Stir in the cheese and chips.

3. Heat the remaining picante sauce in a 1-quart saucepan over medium heat until it's hot. Spoon over the eggs. Top with the avocado. Serve immediately.

**Makes:
4 servings**

**Nutritional
Values Per
Serving:**
Calories 501,
Fat 37g,
Saturated Fat 14g,
Cholesterol 463mg,
Sodium 939mg,
Carbohydrate 22g,
Fiber 7g,
Protein 22g

Picante Brunch Quiche

Start to Finish: 55 minutes
Prep: 10 minutes **Bake:** 35 minutes
Stand: 10 minutes

1 cup shredded Cheddar cheese (4 ounces)
4 slices bacon, cooked and crumbled
2 medium green onions, sliced (about 2 tablespoons)
1 (9-inch) frozen pie crust
½ cup Pace® Picante Sauce
3 eggs
½ cup half-and-half *or* milk

1. Heat the oven to 375°F. Put the cheese, bacon and onions in the pie crust.

2. Beat the picante sauce, eggs and half-and-half with a whisk or fork in a medium bowl. Pour over the cheese mixture.

3. Bake for 35 minutes or until crust is golden and a knife inserted in the center comes out clean. Let the quiche stand for 10 minutes before serving.

Makes: 6 servings

Nutritional Values Per Serving: Calories 283, Fat 20g, Saturated Fat 9g, Cholesterol 139mg, Sodium 591mg, Carbohydrate 13g, Fiber 1g, Protein 11g

Spice Up Your Morning

Huevos Rancheros

Start to Finish: 25 minutes
Prep: 5 minutes
Cook: 20 minutes

½ **cup Pace® Picante Sauce**
1 **teaspoon chili powder**
1 **can (14½ ounces) whole peeled tomatoes, cut up**
1 **tablespoon butter**
8 **eggs**
4 **flour tortillas (8-inch), warmed**

1. Heat the picante sauce, chili powder and tomatoes in a 1-quart saucepan over medium heat until it's hot, stirring often.

2. Heat the butter in a 10-inch skillet over medium heat. Crack **4** of the eggs and add to the skillet one at a time. Cook until the whites are firm or to desired doneness. Remove the eggs with a pancake turner and keep them warm. Repeat with the remaining eggs.

3. Place **2** eggs on each tortilla. Top with picante sauce mixture.

Makes: 4 servings

Nutritional Values Per Serving: Calories 345, Fat 17g, Saturated Fat 6g, Cholesterol 431mg, Sodium 841mg, Carbohydrate 31g, Fiber 4g, Protein 17g

Tomato-Feta Frittata

Start to Finish: 55 minutes
Prep: 15 minutes
Bake: 40 minutes

Vegetable cooking spray
7 eggs
½ cup water
½ cup Pace® Picante Sauce
2 tablespoons chopped fresh cilantro leaves
½ teaspoon dried oregano leaves, crushed
1 cup cooked regular long-grain white rice
¾ cup crumbled feta cheese
½ cup shredded Cheddar cheese
3 Italian plum tomatoes, sliced

1. Heat the oven to 400°F. Spray a 10-inch oven-safe skillet with the cooking spray and place in the oven to heat for about 5 minutes.

2. Beat the eggs and water with a whisk or a fork in a large bowl. Stir in the picante sauce, cilantro, oregano, rice, feta cheese and Cheddar cheese. Pour the egg mixture into the prepared skillet. Top with the tomatoes.

3. Bake for 40 minutes or until a knife inserted in the center comes out clean.

Makes:
6 servings

Nutritional Values Per Serving:
Calories 220,
Fat 13g,
Saturated Fat 7g,
Cholesterol 273mg,
Sodium 518mg,
Carbohydrate 11g,
Fiber 1g,
Protein 13g

Ham Spinach Fiesta Crêpes

Start to Finish: 56 minutes
Prep: 20 minutes Refrigerate: 30 minutes
Microwave: 6 minutes

1½ **cups skim milk**
1⅓ **cups all-purpose flour**
3 **eggs**
1 **jar (15 ounces) Pace® Salsa Con Queso**
1 **package (15 ounces) frozen chopped spinach,
    thawed and well drained**
   Vegetable cooking spray
8 **slices (1 ounce *each*) smoked ham, cut in half**
1 **cup Pace® Chunky Salsa**
1 **cup shredded Cheddar cheese (4 ounces)**

1. Put the milk, flour and eggs in an electric blender container. Cover and blend until smooth. Refrigerate for 30 minutes. Stir the salsa con queso and spinach in a medium bowl. Set aside.

2. Spray a 10-inch nonstick skillet with the cooking spray and heat over medium-high heat for 1 minute. Pour about **3 tablespoons** of the batter into the prepared skillet or crêpe pan, tilting the pan and swirling the batter to cover the bottom. Cook for 1 minute, turning once. Remove the crêpe from the skillet and put on a sheet of waxed paper. Repeat with the remaining batter, making a total of 16 crêpes. (Stack the cooked crêpes between sheets of waxed paper and keep warm.)

3. Place ½ **slice** ham on each crêpe. Top with **3 tablespoons** of the spinach mixture and roll up. Place the filled crêpes into 2 (12×8×2-inch) microwavable shallow baking dishes. Top with the salsa and the cheese. Microwave, one dish at a time, on HIGH for 2 to 3 minutes or until cheese melts.

Time-Saving Tip: To thaw spinach, microwave on HIGH for 3 minutes, breaking apart with a fork halfway through heating.

Makes: 8 servings

Nutritional Values Per Serving:
Calories 390, Fat 19g, Saturated Fat 9g, Cholesterol 127mg, Sodium 1381mg, Carbohydrate 33g, Fiber 3g, Protein 20g

Hot 'n' Honeyed Chicken Wings

Start to Finish: 1 hour, 5 minutes
Prep: 10 minutes
Bake: 55 minutes

1 cup Pace® Picante Sauce
¼ cup honey
½ teaspoon ground ginger
12 chicken wings *or* chicken drummettes

1. Stir the picante sauce, honey and ginger in a small bowl.

2. Cut the chicken wings at the joints into 24 pieces. Discard the tips or save them for another use. Put the wings in a small bowl. Add the picante sauce mixture and toss to coat. Put the wings on a foil-lined shallow baking pan.

3. Bake at 400°F. for 55 minutes or until the wings are glazed and cooked through*, turning and brushing often with sauce during the last 30 minutes of cooking.

*The internal temperature of the chicken should reach 170°F.

Makes: 24 appetizers

Nutritional Values Per Wing: Calories 63, Fat 3g, Saturated Fat 1g, Cholesterol 14mg, Sodium 97mg, Carbohydrate 4g, Fiber 0g, Protein 5g

Tomato-Corn Salsa

Start to Finish: 5 minutes
Prep: 5 minutes

1 jar (16 ounces) Pace® Chunky Salsa
1 cup thawed frozen *or* canned whole kernel corn
  Tortilla chips *or* grilled meats, tacos or fajitas

1. Stir the salsa and corn in a small bowl.

2. Serve with chips for dipping or use as a topping for grilled meats, tacos or fajitas.

Makes: 2 cups

Nutritional Values Per 2 Tablespoons: Calories 13, Fat 0g, Saturated Fat 0g, Cholesterol 0mg, Sodium 204mg, Carbohydrate 3g, Fiber 1g, Protein 0g

Double Cheese Crab Dip

Start to Finish: 20 minutes
Prep: 5 minutes
Bake: 15 minutes

1 **cup Pace® Picante Sauce *or* Chunky Salsa**
1 **teaspoon chili powder**
1 **package (8 ounces) cream cheese, softened**
1 **can (8 ounces) refrigerated pasteurized crabmeat**
1 **cup shredded Cheddar cheese (4 ounces)**
¼ **cup sliced pitted ripe olives**
   Pita bread, cut into wedges, tortilla chips *or* assorted cut-up fresh vegetables

1. Stir the picante sauce and chili powder in a small bowl.

2. Spread the cream cheese in a 9-inch pie plate. Top with the picante sauce mixture, crabmeat, Cheddar cheese, olives and additional picante sauce.

3. Bake at 350°F. for 15 minutes or until hot. Serve with pita, chips or vegetables for dipping.

Time-Saving Tip: To soften the cream cheese, remove cheese from wrapper and put on a microwavable plate. Microwave on HIGH for 15 seconds.

Makes: about 3 cups

Nutritional Values Per 2 Tablespoons:
Calories 64,
Fat 5g,
Saturated Fat 3g,
Cholesterol 21mg,
Sodium 175mg,
Carbohydrate 1g,
Fiber 0g,
Protein 3g

Chunky Salsa Cheesecake

Start to Finish: 3 hours, 45 minutes
Prep: 15 minutes Bake: 30 minutes
Refrigerate: 3 hours

1 cup crushed tortilla chips
1 stick (½ cup) butter, melted
2 packages (8 ounces *each*) cream cheese, softened
1 container (16 ounces) sour cream
2 eggs
2 cups shredded Cheddar cheese (8 ounces)
4 medium green onions, chopped (about ½ cup)
1 to 2 cloves garlic, minced
⅛ teaspoon ground black pepper
1 jar (16 ounces) Pace® Chunky *or* Cilantro Chunky Salsa

1. Mix the tortilla chips with the butter in a small bowl. Press the mixture into the bottom of a 9-inch springform pan. Put the prepared pan on a shallow-sided baking pan.

2. Beat the cream cheese, sour cream and eggs in a medium bowl with an electric mixer at medium speed. Stir in the cheese, onions, garlic and black pepper. Pour into the prepared pan.

3. Bake at 350°F. for 30 minutes or until the center is set. Cool the cheesecake on a wire rack. Cover and refrigerate at least 3 hours before serving. Run a sharp knife around the edges of the springform pan and remove the side. Top with the salsa. Cut into wedges to serve.

Makes:
12 servings

Nutritional
Values Per
Serving:
Calories 418,
Fat 38g,
Saturated Fat 23g,
Cholesterol 134mg,
Sodium 669mg,
Carbohydrate 10g,
Fiber 2g,
Protein 10g

Ultimate Nachos

Start to Finish: *20 minutes*
Prep/Cook: 20 minutes

1	**pound ground beef**
¾	**cup water**
1	**package (1.1 ounces) Pace™ Taco Seasoning**
1	**can (15.6 ounces) Pace™ Traditional Refried Beans**
5	**cups tortilla chips**
2	**cups Pace® Chunky Salsa**
1	**cup shredded Cheddar cheese (4 ounces)**
⅓	**cup drained Pace™ Jalapeños-Nacho Sliced Peppers**

1. Cook the beef in a 10-inch skillet over medium-high heat until the beef is well browned, stirring frequently to break up meat. Pour off any fat. Stir the water and taco seasoning into the skillet. Heat to a boil. Reduce the heat to low. Cook and stir for 5 minutes.

2. Heat the beans according to the package directions.

3. Place the chips on a large platter. Layer the beef mixture, beans, salsa, cheese and peppers over the chips.

Makes: 8 appetizers

Nutritional Values Per Serving: Calories 299, Fat 15g, Saturated Fat 6g, Cholesterol 48mg, Sodium 1358mg, Carbohydrate 23g, Fiber 6g, Protein 17g

Southwest Meatballs

Start to Finish: 1 hour
Prep: 30 minutes
Bake/Cook: 30 minutes

- **2 slices white bread, torn into small pieces**
- **½ cup milk**
- **2 pounds ground beef**
- **2 eggs, beaten**
- **½ teaspoon ground black pepper**
- **1 small onion, finely chopped (about ¼ cup)**
- **3 cloves garlic, minced**
- **¼ cup finely chopped fresh parsley**
- **50 pimiento-stuffed Spanish olives**
- **2 jars (16 ounces *each*) Pace® Picante Sauce**

1. Put the bread in a large bowl with the milk and let soak until the liquid is absorbed. Add the beef, eggs, black pepper, onion, garlic and parsley.

2. Thoroughly mix the ingredients. Shape the mixture firmly into 50 (1-inch) meatballs, placing **1** olive in the center of each meatball. Put the meatballs in a 13×9×2-inch shallow baking dish. Bake at 350°F. for 25 minutes or until meatballs are cooked through*.

3. Remove the meatballs with a slotted spoon and put in a 4-quart saucepot. Add the picante sauce. Cook over medium heat until hot and bubbling. Serve with toothpicks.

*The internal temperature of the meatballs should reach 160°F.

Makes: 50 appetizers

Nutritional Values Per Meatball:
Calories 48,
Fat 3g,
Saturated Fat 1g,
Cholesterol 19mg,
Sodium 246mg,
Carbohydrate 2g,
Fiber 1g,
Protein 4g

Spicy Grilled Quesadillas

Start to Finish: 17 minutes
Prep: 10 minutes **Grill:** 5 minutes
Stand: 2 minutes

- **8 flour tortillas (8-inch)**
- **2 cups shredded Cheddar cheese (8 ounces)**
- **1 jar (16 ounces) Pace® Chunky Salsa (any flavor)**
- **1 cup diced cooked chicken**
- **4 medium green onions, chopped (about ½ cup)**
  Vegetable oil
- **1 container (8 ounces) sour cream**

1. Put **4** of the tortillas on a work surface. Top each with ½ **cup** of the cheese, ¼ **cup** of the salsa, ¼ **cup** of the chicken and **2 tablespoons** of the green onions. Top with the remaining tortillas.

2. Lightly oil the grill rack and heat the grill to medium. Brush the tops of the quesadillas with oil. Place the quesadillas oil-side down on the grill rack. Grill for about 3 minutes. Brush the tops of the quesadillas with oil. Turn and grill for about 2 minutes more or until lightly browned. Remove the quesadillas from the grill and let them stand for 2 minutes.

3. Cut the quesadillas into wedges. Serve with the remaining salsa and sour cream.

Makes: 4 servings

Nutritional Values Per Serving:
Calories 817,
Fat 44g,
Saturated Fat 22g,
Cholesterol 116mg,
Sodium 1815mg,
Carbohydrate 69g,
Fiber 8g,
Protein 35g

Creamy Salsa Dip

Start to Finish: 35 minutes
Prep: 5 minutes
Refrigerate: 30 minutes

1 **jar (16 ounces) Pace® Chunky Salsa**
1 **container (8 ounces) sour cream**
 Assorted cut-up fresh vegetables *and/or*
 tortilla chips

1. Stir the salsa and sour cream in a small bowl.

2. Refrigerate the mixture for 30 minutes or until the flavors
are blended.

3. Serve with the vegetables and chips for dipping.

Makes: 2½ cups

Nutritional Values Per 2 Tablespoons: Calories 31, Fat 2g, Saturated Fat 1g,
Cholesterol 5mg, Sodium 169mg, Carbohydrate 2g, Fiber 1g, Protein 0g

Salsa-Ranch Dip

Start to Finish: 1 hour, 5 minutes
Prep: 5 minutes
Refrigerate: 1 hour

¾ **cup Pace® Chunky Salsa *or* Picante Sauce**
1 **container (16 ounces) sour cream**
1 **package (1.0 ounce) ranch dip mix**
Tortilla chips *or* assorted cut-up fresh vegetables

1. Stir the salsa, sour cream and dip mix in a small bowl.

2. Refrigerate for at least 1 hour until the flavors are blended.

3. Serve with chips or vegetables for dipping.

Makes: 2½ cups

Nutritional Values Per 2 Tablespoons: Calories 56, Fat 5g, Saturated Fat 3g, Cholesterol 10mg, Sodium 249mg, Carbohydrate 2g, Fiber 0g, Protein 1g

Sausage Stuffed Mushrooms

Start to Finish: 35 minutes
Prep: 25 minutes
Bake: 10 minutes

24 medium mushrooms
2 tablespoons butter, melted
4 ounces bulk pork sausage
1 cup Pace® Picante Sauce
½ cup dry bread crumbs
Chopped fresh cilantro *or* parsley

1. Remove the stems from the mushrooms. Chop enough stems to make **1 cup**. Brush the mushroom caps with the butter and set the caps topside down in a shallow baking pan.

2. Cook the sausage and mushroom stems in a 10-inch skillet over medium-high heat until the sausage is well browned, stirring frequently to break up the meat. Stir in **½ cup** of the picante sauce and bread crumbs. Spoon about **1 tablespoon** of the sausage mixture into each mushroom cap.

3. Bake at 425°F. for 10 minutes or until hot and the sausage mixture reaches an internal temperature of 160°F. Top each mushroom with **1 teaspoon** of the remaining picante sauce and cilantro.

Makes:
24 appetizers

Nutritional Values Per Appetizer:
Calories 33,
Fat 2g,
Saturated Fat 1g,
Cholesterol 5mg,
Sodium 126mg,
Carbohydrate 3g,
Fiber 1g,
Protein 1g

Marinated
Picante Chicken

Start to Finish: 50 minutes
Prep: 5 minutes **Marinate:** 30 minutes
Grill: 15 minutes

4 to 6 skinless, boneless chicken breast halves
1 jar (16 ounces) Pace® Picante Sauce

1. Place chicken in a 12×8×2-inch shallow, nonmetallic dish or gallon-size resealable plastic bag. Add **1 cup** of the picante sauce and turn the chicken to coat with the picante sauce. Cover the dish or seal the bag and refrigerate it for 30 minutes, turning over a few times while it's marinating.

2. Lightly oil the grill rack and heat the grill to medium. Remove the chicken from the marinade. Throw away any remaining marinade. Grill the chicken for 15 minutes or until the chicken is cooked through*, turning chicken halfway through cooking and brushing it often with ½ **cup** additional picante sauce.

3. Serve the chicken with remaining picante sauce.

*The internal temperature of the chicken should reach 160°F.

Makes: 6 servings

Nutritional Values Per Serving: Calories 158, Fat 3g, Saturated Fat 1g, Cholesterol 69mg, Sodium 651mg, Carbohydrate 5g, Fiber 2g, Protein 25g

Texas Two-Step
Chicken Picante

Start to Finish: 25 minutes
Prep: 5 minutes
Bake: 20 minutes

4 to 6 skinless, boneless chicken breast halves
1½ cups Pace® Picante Sauce or Chunky Salsa
3 tablespoons packed light brown sugar
1 tablespoon Dijon-style mustard
Hot cooked rice

1. Put the chicken in a 12×8×2-inch shallow baking dish.

2. Stir the picante sauce, brown sugar and mustard in a small bowl. Pour over the chicken.

3. Bake at 400°F. for 20 minutes or until the chicken is cooked through*. Serve with the rice.

*The internal temperature of the chicken should reach 160°F.

Makes: 6 servings

Nutritional Values Per Serving: Calories 367, Fat 4g, Saturated Fat 1g, Cholesterol 73mg, Sodium 861mg, Carbohydrate 50g, Fiber 4g, Protein 30g

Sweet 'n' Spicy Barbecued Brisket

Start to Finish: 12 hours, 50 minutes
Prep: 10 minutes **Marinate**: 8 hours
Cook: 4 hours, 30 minutes **Stand**: 10 minutes

	5-pound trimmed beef brisket
	Ground black pepper
1	tablespoon garlic powder
2	cups Pace® Chunky *or* Chipotle Chunky Salsa
½	cup packed brown sugar
½	cup Worcestershire sauce
10	round sandwich *or* hamburger rolls, split
	Prepared coleslaw

1. Season the brisket with the black pepper and garlic powder and place in a 13×9×2-inch shallow baking dish.

2. Stir the salsa, brown sugar and Worcestershire in a small bowl and spread over the brisket. Cover the dish with foil. Refrigerate for at least 8 hours or overnight.

3. Bake, covered, at 300°F. for 4½ hours or until the meat is fork-tender. Remove the brisket from the dish to a cutting board and let it stand for 10 minutes. Thinly slice across the grain or using 2 forks, shred the brisket. Divide the meat and juices among the rolls. Top meat with coleslaw.

Makes:
10 servings

Nutritional Values Per Serving:
Calories 507,
Fat 13g,
Saturated Fat 5g,
Cholesterol 107mg,
Sodium 794mg,
Carbohydrate 40g,
Fiber 3g,
Protein 56g

7-Layer Meatless Tortilla Pie

Start to Finish: 1 hour
Prep: 20 minutes
Bake: 40 minutes

2 cans (about 15 ounces *each*) pinto beans,
 rinsed and drained
1 cup Pace® Picante Sauce
¼ teaspoon garlic powder *or* 2 cloves garlic, minced
2 tablespoons chopped fresh cilantro leaves
1 can (about 15 ounces) black beans, drained
1 small tomato, chopped (about ½ cup)
7 flour tortillas (8-inch)
2 cups shredded Cheddar cheese (8 ounces)

1. Using a fork, mash the pinto beans in a small bowl. Stir in the ¾ **cup** of the picante sauce and garlic powder. Stir the remaining picante sauce, cilantro, black beans and tomato in another small bowl.

2. Place **1** tortilla on a baking sheet. Spread ¾ cup of the pinto bean mixture over tortilla to within ½-inch of edge. Top with ¼ **cup** of the cheese. Top with **1** tortilla and ⅔ cup of the black bean mixture. Top with ¼ **cup** of the cheese. Repeat layers twice more. Top with remaining tortilla and spread with remaining pinto bean mixture. Cover with foil.

3. Bake at 400°F. for 40 minutes or until hot. Uncover. Top with remaining cheese. Cut into wedges. Serve with additional picante sauce and sprinkle with additional cilantro if desired.

Makes: 6 servings

**Nutritional Values
Per Serving:**
Calories 537,
Fat 17g,
Saturated Fat 9g,
Cholesterol 40mg,
Sodium 1253mg,
Carbohydrate 68g,
Fiber 16g,
Protein 26g

Salmon with Pan-Roasted Corn Salsa

Start to Finish: 20 minutes
Prep: 5 minutes
Bake/Cook: 15 minutes

4 fresh salmon fillets (about 1½ pounds)
1 jar (16 ounces) Pace® Chunky Salsa
1 teaspoon olive oil
1 cup frozen whole kernel corn, thawed and drained
1 tablespoon chopped fresh cilantro leaves
1 tablespoon lemon juice

1. Put the salmon in a 17×11-inch roasting pan. Spoon ½ **cup** of the salsa over the fish.

2. Bake at 400°F. for 15 minutes or until the fish flakes easily when tested with a fork.

3. Heat the oil in an 8-inch nonstick skillet. Add the corn and cook for 4 minutes or until the corn starts to brown. Stir the remaining salsa, cilantro and lemon juice into the skillet. Cook until hot. Serve the salmon with the corn salsa.

Time-Saving Tip: To thaw corn, microwave on HIGH for 1 minute.

Makes: 4 servings

Nutritional Values Per Serving: Calories 361, Fat 19g, Saturated Fat 4g, Cholesterol 91mg, Sodium 904mg, Carbohydrate 11g, Fiber 4g, Protein 32g

Wild West
Picante Burgers

Start to Finish: 15 minutes
Prep: 5 minutes
Grill: 10 minutes

- **1**   **pound ground beef**
- **½**   **cup Pace® Picante Sauce *or* Chunky Salsa**
- **4**   **hamburger rolls, split**

1. Thoroughly mix the beef and picante sauce in a medium bowl. Shape the mixture into 4 (½-inch thick) burgers.

2. Lightly oil the grill rack and heat the grill to medium. Grill the burgers for 10 minutes for medium* or until to desired doneness, turning the burgers over halfway through cooking and brushing them often with additional picante sauce while they're cooking.

3. Serve the burgers in the rolls with additional picante sauce.

The internal temperature of the burgers should reach 160°F.

Makes: 4 sandwiches

Nutritional Values Per Sandwich: Calories 323, Fat 13g, Saturated Fat 5g, Cholesterol 71mg, Sodium 522mg, Carbohydrate 23g, Fiber 2g, Protein 25g

Tijuana
T-Bones

Start to Finish: 1 hour, 22 minutes
Prep: 10 minutes **Marinate:** 1 hour
Grill: 12 minutes

1½	cups Pace® Chunky Salsa
2½	teaspoons ground cumin
4	T-bone steaks (about 8 ounces *each*), ½-inch thick
2	tablespoons fresh lime juice
¼	cup chopped fresh cilantro leaves
1	can (about 15 ounces) black beans, rinsed and drained
1	large avocado, peeled, seeded and chopped (about 1½ cups)

1. Stir **1 cup** of the salsa and **2 teaspoons** of the cumin in a 13×9×2-inch shallow, nonmetallic dish or gallon-size resealable plastic bag. Add the steaks and turn them over to coat with the marinade. Cover the dish or seal the plastic bag and refrigerate it for 1 hour, turning the steaks over a few times while they're marinating.

2. Stir the remaining salsa, remaining cumin, lime juice, cilantro, beans and avocado in a medium bowl and set aside.

3. Lightly oil the grill rack and heat the grill to medium. Remove the steaks from the marinade. Throw away any remaining marinade. Grill the steaks for 12 minutes for medium-rare* or to desired doneness, turning the steaks over halfway through cooking. Serve the steaks with the salsa mixture.

*The internal temperature of the meat should reach 145°F.

Makes:
4 servings

Nutritional Values Per Serving:
Calories 500,
Fat 21g,
 Saturated Fat 6g,
 Cholesterol 79mg,
 Sodium 983mg,
 Carbohydrate 30g,
 Fiber 13g,
 Protein 46g

Black Bean, Corn & Turkey Chili

Start to Finish: 50 minutes
Prep: 5 minutes
Cook: 45 minutes

 1 tablespoon vegetable oil
 1 pound ground turkey
 1 large onion, chopped (about 1 cup)
 2 tablespoons chili powder
 1 teaspoon ground cumin
 1 teaspoon dried oregano leaves, crushed
 ½ teaspoon ground black pepper
 ¼ teaspoon garlic powder *or* 2 cloves garlic, minced
1¾ cups Swanson® Chicken Broth (Regular,
       Natural Goodness™ or Certified Organic)
 1 cup Pace® Chunky Salsa
 1 tablespoon sugar
 1 can (about 15 ounces) black beans, rinsed and drained
 1 can (16 ounces) whole kernel corn, drained

1. Heat the oil in a 4-quart saucepan over medium-high heat. Add the turkey, onion, chili powder, cumin, oregano, black pepper and garlic powder. Cook until turkey is well browned, stirring frequently to break up meat.

2. Stir the broth, salsa, sugar, beans and corn into the saucepan. Heat to a boil. Reduce the heat to low.

3. Cover and cook for 30 minutes. Stir the chili occasionally while cooking.

Makes:
6 servings

**Nutritional
Values
Per Serving:**
Calories 301,
Fat 11g,
Saturated Fat 2g,
Cholesterol 57mg,
Sodium 884mg,
Carbohydrate 31g,
Fiber 8g,
Protein 22g

Picante Skillet Chicken

Start to Finish: 25 minutes
Prep: 5 minutes
Cook: 20 minutes

1 **tablespoon vegetable oil**
4 **to 6 skinless, boneless chicken breast halves**
1 **jar (16 ounces) Pace® Picante Sauce**
   Hot cooked rice

1. Heat the oil in a 10-inch skillet over medium-high heat. Add the chicken and cook for 10 minutes or until it's well browned on both sides.

2. Add the picante sauce to the skillet. Heat to a boil. Reduce the heat to medium. Cover and cook for 5 minutes or until the chicken is cooked through*.

3. Serve with the rice.

The internal temperature of the chicken should reach 160°F.

Makes: 6 servings

Nutritional Values Per Serving: Calories 384, Fat 6g, Saturated Fat 1g, Cholesterol 69mg, Sodium 653mg, Carbohydrate 49g, Fiber 3g, Protein 30g

Grilled Citrus Chicken with Black Bean Salsa

Start to Finish: 40 minutes
Prep: 10 minutes   **Marinate:** 20 minutes
Grill: 10 minutes

- **3** tablespoons lemon juice
- **2** tablespoons olive oil
- **⅓** cup chopped fresh cilantro leaves
- **2** cloves garlic, minced
- **¼** teaspoon crushed red pepper
- **4** to 6 skinless, boneless chicken breast halves
- **1** jar (16 ounces) Pace® Chunky Salsa
- **1** can (about 15 ounces) black beans, rinsed and drained

1. Stir **2 tablespoons** of the lemon juice, oil, **3 tablespoons** of the cilantro, garlic and red pepper in a 13×9×2-inch shallow, nonmetallic baking dish or gallon-size resealable plastic bag. Add the chicken and turn it over to coat with the marinade. Cover the dish or seal the plastic bag and refrigerate it for 20 minutes, turning the chicken over a few times while it's marinating.

2. Stir the remaining lemon juice, remaining cilantro, salsa and beans in a small bowl and set aside.

3. Lightly oil the grill rack and heat the grill to medium. Remove the chicken from the marinade. Throw away any remaining marinade. Grill the chicken for 10 minutes or until the chicken is cooked through*, turning the chicken over halfway through cooking. Serve the chicken with the salsa mixture.

*The internal temperature of the chicken should reach 160°F.

Makes: 6 servings

Nutritional Values Per Serving:
Calories 336,
Fat 10g,
Saturated Fat 2g,
Cholesterol 73mg,
Sodium 1051mg,
Carbohydrate 26g,
Fiber 10g,
Protein 33g

Grilled Picante
Beef & Vegetable Wraps

Start to Finish: 35 minutes
Prep: 20 minutes
Grill: 15 minutes

- ⅔ cup mayonnaise
- ½ cup Pace® Chunky *or* Cilantro Chunky Salsa
- ⅓ cup chopped fresh cilantro leaves
- 1 tablespoon lime juice
- ½ teaspoon ground cumin
- ¼ teaspoon crushed red pepper
- ¼ teaspoon celery seed
- 1½ cups shredded cabbage
- ⅓ cup green pepper, cut in 2-inch-long strips
- 1¾ pounds ground beef
- 1 cup Pace® Picante Sauce
- ¾ cup crushed corn chips
- 2 medium green onions, chopped (about ¼ cup)
- ¾ cup shredded Pepper Jack cheese
- 6 flour tortillas (10-inch)

1. Stir the mayonnaise, salsa, cilantro, lime juice, cumin, red pepper and celery seed in a medium bowl. Add the cabbage and green pepper, tossing until well coated. Cover and refrigerate until serving time.

2. Thoroughly mix the beef, picante sauce, chips, green onions and cheese in a medium bowl. Shape the mixture into 6 (7-inch long and 2-inch thick) burgers.

3. Lightly oil the grill rack and heat the grill to medium. Grill the burgers for 12 minutes for medium* or to desired doneness, turning the burgers over halfway through cooking. Keep warm.

4. Wrap the tortillas in foil. Grill the tortillas for 3 minutes or until they're warm. Put the tortillas on the work surface. Put the burger in the center of each tortilla. Divide the cabbage mixture among the burgers. Roll up each tortilla to enclose the filling. Slice the wrap diagonally in half.

*The internal temperature of the burgers should reach 145°F.

Makes: 6 wraps

Nutritional Values Per Wrap:
Calories 745, Fat 45g, Saturated Fat 13g,
Cholesterol 110mg, Sodium 1303mg,
Carbohydrate 48g, Fiber 5g, Protein 34g

Kick Up Your Meals

Orange Picante Pork Chops

Start to Finish: 1 hour, 20 minutes
Prep: 5 minutes **Marinate:** 1 hour
Grill: 15 minutes

¾ **cup Pace® Picante Sauce**
¼ **cup orange juice**
¼ **teaspoon garlic powder *or* 2 cloves garlic, minced**
4 **boneless pork chops, ¾-inch thick**

1. Stir the picante sauce, orange juice and garlic powder in a 12×8×2-inch shallow, nonmetallic dish or gallon-size resealable plastic bag. Add the chops and turn them to coat with the picante sauce mixture. Cover the dish or seal the plastic bag and refrigerate for 1 hour, turning the chops over a few times while they're marinating.

2. Lightly oil the grill rack and heat the grill to medium. Remove the chops from the marinade.

3. Grill the chops for 15 minutes or until cooked through but slightly pink in the center*, turning the chops over halfway through cooking and brushing often with marinade while they're grilling. Throw away any remaining marinade.

*The internal temperature of the pork should reach 160°F.

**Makes:
4 servings**

Nutritional Values Per Serving:
Calories 174,
Fat 7g,
Saturated Fat 3g,
Cholesterol 51mg,
Sodium 405mg,
Carbohydrate 5g,
Fiber 2g,
Protein 20g

Shredded BBQ Chicken Sandwiches

Start to Finish: 35 minutes
Prep: 10 minutes
Cook: 25 minutes

2 jars (16 ounces *each*) Pace® Chunky Salsa
1 tablespoon apple cider vinegar
¼ cup packed brown sugar
½ teaspoon garlic powder
¼ teaspoon chili powder
1 pound skinless, boneless chicken breast halves
1 package (13 ounces) Pepperidge Farm®
   Sandwich Buns
   Shredded Cheddar cheese

1. Stir the salsa, vinegar, brown sugar, garlic powder and chili powder in a 4-quart saucepot over medium-high heat to a boil.

2. Add the chicken. Reduce the heat to low. Cover and cook for 20 minutes or until the chicken is cooked through*. Remove from the heat.

3. Remove the chicken with kitchen tongs to a cutting board. Using two forks, shred the chicken. Return the chicken to saucepot. Cook until hot. Divide the chicken mixture among the buns. Sprinkle with the cheese.

*The internal temperature of the chicken should reach 160°F.

Makes: 8 sandwiches

Nutritional Values Per Sandwich:
Calories 315,
Fat 9g,
Saturated Fat 4g,
Cholesterol 48mg,
Sodium 1154mg,
Carbohydrate 36g,
Fiber 5g,
Protein 21g

Salsa BBQ Chicken Lettuce Wraps

Start to Finish: 1 hour, 30 minutes
Prep/Grill: 30 minutes
Marinate: 1 hour

1¼	cups Pace® Chunky *or* Chipotle Chunky Salsa
4	to 6 skinless, boneless chicken breast halves
4	large romaine *or* iceberg lettuce leaves
2	medium carrots, shredded (about 1 cup)
2	stalks celery, sliced (about ½ cup)
¼	cup crumbled blue cheese (about 1 ounce)

1. Pour ½ **cup** of the salsa into a 12×8×2-inch shallow, nonmetallic dish or gallon-size resealable plastic bag. Add the chicken and turn it over to coat with the salsa. Cover the dish or seal the bag and refrigerate for 1 hour, turning the chicken over a few times while it's marinating.

2. Lightly oil the grill rack and heat the grill to medium. Remove the chicken from marinade. Throw away any remaining marinade. Grill the chicken for 10 minutes or until the chicken is cooked through*, turning the chicken over halfway through cooking and brushing the chicken often with ¼ **cup** of the salsa while it's grilling. Remove the chicken from grill to a cutting board and let it stand for 5 minutes. Thinly slice the chicken breasts.

3. Put lettuce leaves on the work surface. Arrange ¼ of the sliced chicken down the center of each lettuce leaf. Top the chicken with ¼ **cup** of the carrots, **2 tablespoons** of the celery, **2 tablespoons** of the salsa and **1 tablespoon** of the cheese. Roll up each lettuce leaf to enclose the filling. Serve immediately.

*The internal temperature of the chicken should reach 160°F.

Makes: 4 wraps

Nutritional Values Per Wrap:
Calories 204,
Fat 5g,
Saturated Fat 2g,
Cholesterol 76mg,
Sodium 733mg,
Carbohydrate 11g,
Fiber 4g,
Protein 28g

Grilled Stuffed Pork with Fruit Salsa

Start to Finish: 1 hour
Prep: 20 minutes **Cook/Grill:** 30 minutes
Stand: 10 minutes

1	whole pork tenderloin (1½ pounds), butterflied
1	cup Pace® Chunky *or* Chipotle Chunky Salsa
7½	ounces cooked chorizo sausage *or* pepperoni, chopped (about 2 cups)
½	cup Pepperidge Farm® Garlic Herb Croutons, crushed
1	cup orange juice
3	tablespoons chopped fresh cilantro leaves
2	tablespoons packed brown sugar
1	ripe mango, peeled, seeded and chopped (about 1½ cups)

1. Put the pork between 2 sheets of plastic wrap. Working from the center, pound the pork flat into a 14×6-inch rectangle. Remove the plastic wrap. Stir ½ **cup** of the salsa, the chorizo and croutons in a medium bowl. Spread the chorizo mixture lengthwise down the center of the pork. Fold the sides over the filling to form a 14-inch long roll. Tie the pork crosswise at 2-inch intervals with kitchen twine.

2. Add the remaining salsa, orange juice, cilantro, brown sugar and mango to an electric blender or food processor container. Cover and blend the mixture until it's smooth and pour into a 10-inch skillet. Heat over medium-high heat to a boil. Reduce the heat to medium-low. Cook and stir for 20 minutes or until the sauce thickens.

3. Lightly oil the grill rack and heat the grill to medium. Grill the pork for 20 to 30 minutes or until cooked through but slightly pink*, turning the pork over halfway through cooking. Remove the pork from the grill and let stand 10 minutes. Thinly slice the pork and serve with the mango sauce.

*The internal temperature of the pork should reach 155°F. During the standing time the temperature will continue to increase to 160°F.

Makes: 6 servings

Nutritional Values Per Serving: Calories 418, Fat 22g, Saturated Fat 8g, Cholesterol 97mg, Sodium 1156mg, Carbohydrate 21g, Fiber 2g, Protein 32g

Grilled Picante
BBQ Chicken

Start to Finish: 20 minutes
Prep: 5 minutes
Grill: 15 minutes

¾ **cup Pace® Picante Sauce**
¼ **cup prepared barbecue sauce**
4 **to 6 skinless, boneless chicken breast halves**

1. Stir the picante sauce and the barbecue sauce in a small bowl. Reserve ½ **cup** of the picante sauce mixture.

2. Lightly oil the grill rack and heat the grill to medium. Grill the chicken for 15 minutes or until chicken is cooked through*, turning the chicken halfway through and brushing it often with the remaining picante mixture while it's grilling. Throw away any remaining picante sauce mixture.

3. Serve the chicken with the reserved picante sauce.

*The internal temperature of the chicken should reach 160°F.

Makes: 6 servings

Nutritional Values Per Serving: Calories 153, Fat 3g, Saturated Fat 1g, Cholesterol 69mg, Sodium 395mg, Carbohydrate 3g, Fiber 1g, Protein 26g

Baked Potatoes Olé

Start to Finish: 20 minutes
Prep/Cook: 20 minutes

1 **pound ground beef**
1 **tablespoon chili powder**
1 **cup Pace® Picante Sauce**
4 **hot baked potatoes, split**
 Shredded Cheddar cheese

1. Cook the beef and chili powder in a 10-inch skillet over medium-high heat until the beef is well browned, stirring frequently to break up meat. Pour off any fat.

2. Stir the picante sauce into the skillet. Reduce the heat to low. Cook until hot and bubbling.

3. Serve over the potatoes. Top with cheese.

Makes: 4 servings

Nutritional Values Per Serving: Calories 434, Fat 17g, Saturated Fat 7g, Cholesterol 82mg, Sodium 690mg, Carbohydrate 42g, Fiber 6g, Protein 29g

Shrimp 'n' Shells Salad

Start to Finish: 2 hours, 25 minutes
Prep: 25 minutes
Refrigerate: 2 hours

2¼	**cups medium shell-shaped pasta, cooked and drained**
1	**medium green pepper, cut into 2-inch-long strips (about 1½ cups)**
1½	**cups cherry tomatoes, cut in half**
2	**medium green onions, sliced (about ¼ cup)**
1	**pound medium shrimp, cooked, shelled and deveined**
⅔	**cup Pace® Picante Sauce**
⅓	**cup mayonnaise**
¼	**cup chopped fresh cilantro leaves**
¾	**teaspoon ground cumin**

1. Stir the pasta, pepper, cherry tomatoes, green onions and shrimp in a large bowl.

2. Beat the picante sauce, mayonnaise, cilantro and cumin with a whisk or fork in a small bowl. Pour over the pasta mixture, tossing until well coated.

3. Cover and refrigerate the salad for at least 2 hours. Stir the salad before serving.

Makes:
4 servings

Nutritional Values Per Serving:
Calories 226,
Fat 11g,
Saturated Fat 2g,
Cholesterol 104mg,
Sodium 407mg,
Carbohydrate 19g,
Fiber 2g,
Protein 13g

Best-of-the-West Bean Salad

Start to Finish: 2 hours, 10 minutes
Prep: 10 minutes
Refrigerate: 2 hours

1 **large green pepper, diced (about 1 cup)**
1 **medium red onion, very thinly sliced**
1 **can (about 15 ounces) kidney beans, rinsed and drained**
1 **can (about 15 ounces) pinto beans, rinsed and drained**
¾ **cup Pace® Picante Sauce**
2 **tablespoons red wine vinegar**
1 **tablespoon vegetable oil**
2 **tablespoons chopped fresh cilantro leaves**

1. Stir the pepper, red onion and beans in a medium bowl.

2. Beat the picante sauce, vinegar, oil and cilantro with a whisk or fork in a small bowl. Pour the dressing over the salad mixture, tossing until lightly coated.

3. Cover and refrigerate the salad for at least 2 hours. Stir the salad before serving. Garnish with additional cilantro.

Makes: 8 servings

Nutritional Values Per Serving:
Calories 131,
Fat 2g,
Saturated Fat 0g,
Cholesterol 0mg,
Sodium 361mg,
Carbohydrate 22g,
Fiber 7g,
Protein 6g

Fettuccine Picante

Start to Finish: 25 minutes
Prep: 20 minutes
Cook: 5 minutes

- ½ **cup Pace® Picante Sauce**
- ½ **cup sour cream**
- ⅓ **cup grated Parmesan cheese**
- ½ **of a 16 ounce package fettuccine pasta, cooked and drained**
- 2 **tablespoons chopped fresh cilantro leaves**

1. Heat the picante sauce, sour cream and cheese in a 1-quart saucepan over low heat. Cook and stir until hot.

2. Place the pasta and cilantro in a medium serving bowl. Pour the picante sauce mixture over the pasta, tossing until well coated.

3. Serve with additional picante sauce.

Makes: 4 servings

Nutritional Values Per Serving: Calories 305, Fat 9g, Saturated Fat 5g, Cholesterol 20mg, Sodium 393mg, Carbohydrate 43g, Fiber 3g, Protein 11g

Avocado Melon Salad & Picante Honey Dressing

Start to Finish: 20 minutes
Prep: 20 minutes

- **3** cups spinach leaves torn in bite-size pieces
- **2** cups cubed cantaloupe
- **1** large avocado, peeled, pitted and cut into cubes
- **½** cup Pace® Picante Sauce
- **3** tablespoons honey
- **2** tablespoons lime juice
- **1** tablespoon vegetable oil
- **¼** cup toasted slivered blanched almonds

1. Stir the spinach, cantaloupe and avocado in a large bowl.

2. Beat the picante sauce, honey, lime juice and oil with a whisk or fork in a small bowl. Pour the dressing over the salad mixture, tossing until lightly coated.

3. Sprinkle with the almonds. Serve immediately.

TIP: To toast the almonds, arrange the almonds in a single layer in a shallow baking pan. Bake at 350°F. for 10 minutes or until lightly browned.

Makes: 6 servings

Nutritional Values Per Serving:
Calories 171,
Fat 10g,
Saturated Fat 1g,
Cholesterol 0mg,
Sodium 192mg,
Carbohydrate 19g,
Fiber 4g,
Protein 3g

Cornbread Squares

Start to Finish: 30 minutes
Prep: 10 minutes
Bake: 20 minutes

Vegetable cooking spray
1 package (about 8 ounces) corn muffin mix
½ cup Pace® Picante Sauce
½ cup shredded Cheddar cheese

1. Heat the oven to 400°F. Spray an 8-inch square baking pan with the cooking spray.

2. Prepare the corn muffin mix according to the package directions. Spread **half** of the batter in the prepared pan. Top with the picante sauce and cheese. Spread the remaining batter on top.

3. Bake for 20 minutes or until a toothpick inserted in the center comes out clean.

Makes: 9 servings

Nutritional Values Per Serving: Calories 135, Fat 5g, Saturated Fat 2g, Cholesterol 7mg, Sodium 430mg, Carbohydrate 18g, Fiber 2g, Protein 3g

Firehouse
Salsa Bars

Start to Finish: 1 hour, 55 minutes
Prep: 15 minutes **Bake:** 40 minutes
Cool: 1 hour

½ **of a large ripe banana, cut up (about 1 cup)**
1 **cup Pace® Chunky Salsa**
½ **cup apricot preserves**
1 **teaspoon cornstarch**
2 **sticks (1 cup) butter, softened**
1 **cup packed brown sugar**
1½ **teaspoons vanilla extract**
½ **teaspoon ground allspice**
2 **cups self-rising flour**
1 **cup coarsely crushed gingersnap cookies**
1 **cup quick-cooking oats**

1. Heat the oven to 350°F. Put the banana, salsa, preserves and cornstarch in a food processor container. Cover and pulse for 30 seconds or until smooth. Set aside.

2. Beat the butter, brown sugar, vanilla and allspice in a large bowl with an electric mixer at medium speed until the mixture is light and fluffy. Add the flour, cookie crumbs and oats. Beat until crumbly. Reserve ⅓ **cup** of the crumb mixture for the topping. Press remaining crumb mixture in a 13×9×2-inch baking pan. Top with the salsa mixture. Sprinkle with the reserved crumb mixture.

3. Bake for 40 minutes or until brown. Cool in the pan on a wire rack. Cut into 24 (about 2×2-inch) bars.

Makes:
24 bars

Nutritional Values Per Bar:
Calories 193,
Fat 8g,
Saturated Fat 5g,
Cholesterol 20mg,
Sodium 303mg,
Carbohydrate 28g,
Fiber 1g,
Protein 2g

Corn and Black-Eyed Pea Salad

Start to Finish: 4 hours, 15 minutes
Prep: 15 minutes
Refrigerate: 4 hours

1 bag (16 ounces) frozen whole kernel corn, thawed (about 3 cups)
1 can (about 15 ounces) black-eyed peas, rinsed and drained
1 large green pepper, chopped (about 1 cup)
½ cup chopped red onion
½ cup chopped fresh cilantro leaves
1 jar (16 ounces) Pace® Chunky Salsa

1. Stir the corn, peas, green pepper, red onion and cilantro in a medium bowl. Stir the salsa into the corn mixture until well coated.

2. Cover and refrigerate the salad for 4 hours.

3. Stir the salad before serving.

Cooking for a Crowd: Recipe may be doubled.

Make Ahead: Prepare the salad as directed. Cover and refrigerate the salad overnight. Stir the salad before serving.

Makes: 8 servings

Nutritional Values Per Serving: Calories 113, Fat 1g, Saturated Fat 0g, Cholesterol 0mg, Sodium 503mg, Carbohydrate 25g, Fiber 6g, Protein 3g

Banana Salsa Bread

Start to Finish: 2 hours, 15 minutes
Prep: 15 minutes **Bake:** 1 hour
Cool: 1 hour

Vegetable cooking spray
1   stick (½ cup) butter, softened
1   cup sugar
3   medium ripe bananas, mashed (about 1 cup)
1   cup Pace® Chunky Salsa
2   eggs
2   cups all-purpose flour
1   teaspoon baking soda

1. Heat the oven to 350°F. Spray a 9×5×3-inch loaf pan with cooking spray. Set aside.

2. Beat the butter and sugar in a large bowl with an electric mixer at medium speed until the mixture is light and fluffy. Add the bananas, salsa and eggs and beat until the ingredients are mixed. Reduce the speed to low. Beat in the flour and baking soda just until the ingredients are moistened. Pour the batter into the prepared pan.

3. Bake for 1 hour or until a toothpick inserted in the center comes out clean. Cool in the pan on a wire rack for 15 minutes. Remove from the pan and cool completely on the rack.

Makes:
1 (9-inch) loaf
(16 slices)

Nutritional Values Per Slice:
Calories 191,
Fat 7g,
Saturated Fat 4g,
Cholesterol 42mg, Sodium 204mg, Carbohydrate 31g,
Fiber 1g,
Protein 3g